# Wall Pockets of the Past

**FREDDA PERKINS**

**COLLECTOR BOOKS**

*A Division of Schroeder Publishing Co., Inc.*

The current values in this book should be used only as a guide. They are not intended to set prices, which vary from one section of the country to another. Auction prices as well as dealer prices vary greatly and are affected by condition as well as demand. Neither the Author nor the Publisher assumes responsibility for any losses that might be incurred as a result of consulting this guide.

*Searching For A Publisher?*

We are always looking for knowledgeable people considered to be experts within their fields. If you feel that there is a real need for a book on your collectible subject and have a large comprehensive collection, contact us.

Cover Design:      Beth Summers
Book Design:       Benjamin R. Faust

On the cover from top clockwise:
  •Woman with hat. Unidentified pocket marked USA. Estimated value: $25.00 to $35.00.
  •Man with beard. Unidentified and unmarked. Estimated value: $20.00 to $30.00.
  •Majolica shell. Unmarked, probably English. Estimated value: $250.00 to $375.00.
  •Weller Woodcraft. Marked WELLER. Estimated value: $95.00 to $125.00.
  •Morton Pottery cocketiel. Unmarked. Estimated value: $20.00 to $25.00.
  •Wishing well. Unidentified and unmarked. Estimated value: $10.00 to $15.00

Additional copies of this book may be ordered from:

COLLECTOR BOOKS
P.O. Box 3009
Paducah, KY  42002-3009

@ $17.95. Add $2.00 for postage and handling.

Copyright: Fredda Perkins, 1996

Printed by IMAGE GRAPHICS, INC., Paducah, Kentucky

# Contents

# Acknowledgments

I would like to thank all of the collectors who took their time to write or call me with information for this book. I would especially like to thank all those who took the time to photograph their collections of wall pockets and share them with me. Their assistance has been invaluable in putting together this book. While I was not able to use all the photos submitted, they provided me with new knowledge of sizes, color combinations, and collector's interests. Specifically, I want to thank the following collectors and antique dealers: Mary Jo Brown; Emily Childs; Carol Finch; Joyce Hughes; Julia Kohnovich; Diane Lederer; Rena London; Charlotte Martin; Anita Taylor; my sisters Ellen Musselman and Becky Clem; Jean Williams, owner of the Antique House in McKinney, TX; the dealers of the Antique Company Mall in McKinney, TX; Jimmy Stevenson, owner of McKinney Antiques in McKinney, TX; J.T. and Geraldine Green, dealers in American art pottery, Garland, TX; John Fletcher and Jerry Hayes, dealers in majolica and owners of Fletcher-Hayes, Shell Beach, Calif.; Nickerson's Antiques, Eldon, MO; Jim and Gloria Jordan, owners of Dealers Choice, Kansas City, KS; Larry Pogue, owner of Old Mill Antiques, Jefferson, TX; Lewis Bettinger, dealer in American art pottery; and the dealers of the Unlimited, Ltd. Antique Mall, Dallas, TX.

I would like to especially thank Bobbie and Alan Bryson for sharing their collection of glass wall pockets and their knowledge about that subject, Linda Gilson for sharing her extensive knowledge about McCoy wall pockets as well as her pictures, and Lynn and Ron Tosh for sharing their beautiful collection of Japanese bird wall pockets. Special thanks must also go to Dan Leslie who never saw a wall pocket he didn't like and cheerfully shared his 800 plus collection with me and the readers of this book.

I would like to thank Lisa Tibbals, librarian for the Collin County Community College, for her assistance in finding articles and books for me. I would also like to thank Robert Davis for his suggestions on photography and for taking some of the pictures. Thanks to Ann Mullaney for proofreading this book.

I would especially like to thank my husband, Dan Perkins, for being such a good sport about going to antique malls and shows weekend after weekend and helping me take photographs.

# About the Author

Fredda Moore Perkins has collected wallpockets for sixteen years. She is particularly fond of Japanese luster pockets, especially birds. She is a collector of many other antique and nostaligic items including majolica, beaded bags, miniature metal jewelry boxes, and wicker and American Victorian furniture. She and her husband, Dan Perkins, and her two daughters, Jennifer and Hope, live in McKinney, Texas, in a Victorian home that they have restored. A family of collectors, Dan collects wood and plastic radios from the 30s and 40s, Jennifer collects Murano glass ashtrays from the 50s, and Hope collects Lucite purses from the 40s and 50s.

Fredda has a Ph.D. in psychology and education and is a licensed professional counselor. She works with her psychologist husband in his private practice. She and her husband co-authored a book on habit control and are published in the field of psychology. In addition to her professional work, she writes in the area of collectibles.

# Introduction

"The most creative and exciting thing a collector can do in the antiques market is to find a field about which little has been written and capture the subject for his own private amusement" (Jeremy Cooper in *Dealing With Dealers: The Ins and Outs of the London Antiques Trade*). There are few collectibles for which that quote could be more true than wall pockets. Produced by many manufacturers and craftsmen, wall pockets have been a popular decorative item in the American home since the Victorian era. However, little seems to have been written about them. When mentioned, it is only as a brief aside about curiosities and whimsies. The source of their popularity, especially during the first half of the twentieth century, remains somewhat obscure. This bit of mystery only adds to their charm and challenges collectors to collect more pockets and search for more information.

Wall pockets are the ideal collectible for the individual without much money to spend or without much space for display. Many lovely wall pockets can still be found for about $15.00 at flea markets and antique shops. When found at garage sales, they may be considerably cheaper.

Wall pockets require no shelves, display cases, or albums for preservation. Since they hang on the wall, they can be displayed in a mixed grouping with pictures and photos or hung alone (PLATE 1). They have special impact when a collection is hung as a unit (See PLATES 2, 3, 4). A collection of wall pockets is the perfect decoration on the wall of a guest bath or in a hall. One collector hangs her Roseville and Weller pockets above a table laden with matching vases and bowls of the same make and design. Another collector displays wall pockets with a vegetable and flower motif in her kitchen. Still another collector accents her teapot collection with another collection of teapot shaped wall pockets.

## What is a Wall Pocket?

Actually, wall vase might be a more appropriate name since wall pockets collected today were almost always used to hold flowers. Technically, however, wall pockets can be any wall hung item used to hold something. Yet, most collectors today refer to wall vases as wall pockets despite the fact that most look like some sort of vase with a flat back with a hole in it. An interesting variation on the flat backed pocket is one that was made to fit into a corner (PLATE 5). These are very rare and the author has only found three in her years of collecting. Some wall pockets have flat bot-

PLATE 1. These beautiful Oriental-style wall pockets hold their own against a densely patterned, Victorian wallpaper. They make an attractive grouping with framed masks from China and a large mask from Mexico.

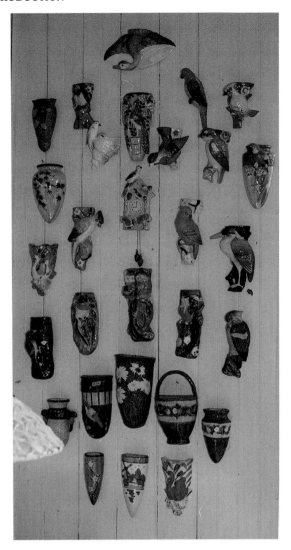

PLATE 3. This collection of miniature pockets graces a narrow space between a door and a jog in a much longer wall. All of these pockets are under five inches, most are three or less. Ironically, often very small pockets are more expensive than larger ones.

PLATE 2. These colorful Japanese pockets brighten an otherwise plain wall in a kitchen. This collection represents a good sample of Japanese bird and flower pockets. Can you spot the lone Czechoslovakian pocket?

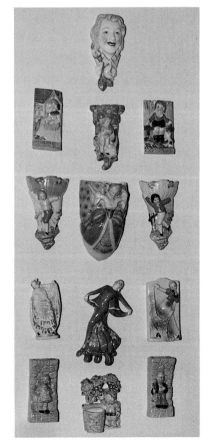

PLATE 4. This collection of pockets fills a narrow wall at the top of a stairs. It has a human theme with most of the subjects being women or children. Adult men are much less common although one finds occasional Indians or men from exotic lands. Royal Copley seemed to produce the most pockets depicting men.

toms to stand them on a surface if they are not to be hung. American manufacturers such as Shawnee and Royal Copley made many pockets that could also be used as free standing planters or vases.

# A Brief History

The early twentieth century wall pocket finds its ancestral roots in the Victorian era. During that time, wall pockets of all kinds were handcrafted to hold a variety of household articles. One enthusiastic writer intoned that ". . . probably no article of modern invention and ingenuity has offered greater satisfaction than wall pockets." (Weed, Clarance M. "The Useful Wallpocket," *House Beautiful*, 1916.) Wall pockets with wooden backs and needle worked fronts were often used to hold house slippers or newspapers in the parlor. More dainty ones, made of cardboard and decorated with ribbon and flowers, might have been used to hold handkerchiefs or jewelry in the bedroom. Generally, these wall pockets were made at home. These handmade wall pockets gave testimony of the artistic prowess of the lady of the house. Unfortunately, few of the unique pockets still exist today. Like many modern crafts, they gradually went out of fashion and were probably thrown away.

Wicker wall pockets were also popular during the Victorian era. They could hold letters or newspapers or dried flower arrangements that were so popular during that era (See PLATES 6 & 7).

The Victorians' enthusiasm for indoor plants may have lead to the initial popularity of wall pockets. During the latter part of the nineteenth century, Victorian homemakers were very fond of growing indoor plants and naturalism was an important design element. Ivy was trained to twine around windows and was often seen cascading from small wall hung shelves. Plants, particularly hanging vines, became such an important decorative item that angled metal planters were fabricated to fit behind wall hung pictures. Pictures were commonly hung in a manner that allowed them to tilt forward and the planter fit in the space behind them. A landscape might then have actual greenery spilling from around the frame. This interest in bringing nature indoors may have led to the manufacture of decorative containers designed specifically to allow plants to become a decoration for the wall.

A type of ceramic that reflected the Victorian interest in nature became very popular in England after the Crystal Palace Exhibition in 1851. This pottery was called majolica after the sixteenth century ware from which it had been copied. Soon its popularity spread to the United States. Among the most beautiful and rather eccentric items produced in majolica were wall pockets. These wall pockets are some of the oldest represented in this book.

Ceramic wall pockets came into vogue after the turn of the century. In a 1916 article entitled "The Useful Wall-Pockets" that appeared in *House Beautiful*, the author enthused, "It is significant that one of the most interesting lines of progress in the recent pottery manufacture has been the production of a great variety of designs of the so-called wall-pockets intended for use on walls or other vertical surfaces." He goes on to report to his readers that ". . . wall-pockets are offered in a great variety of shapes, colors, and decorations by the better shops and department stores of the larger

PLATE 5. These pockets are hung on the sides of kitchen cabinets as they are broken by a window over a sink. Notice the unusual pocket made to fit into a corner. Another corner pocket is displayed on the opposite side of the window.

*PLATE 6. This wicker pocket, decorated with beads, is approximately 12" tall. It probably held letters or perhaps a folded newspaper in a Victorian parlor. It remains as practical today as it was 100 years ago.*

cities, as well as in the catalogues of the more important seed- and plant-houses." The author, Clarence Moores Weed, suggests a wide variety of plants that might be grown and displayed in these pockets. Apparently these early pockets were of ample size because in addition to trailing vines, Mr. Weed includes such spring bulbs as daffodils, hyacinths, and narcissus as appropriate plants for these "useful wall-pockets."

Mr. Weed also provided his readership with some decorating tips. He suggests the following:

"Very attractive combinations of plant and picture may be made by hanging the wall-pockets in connection with appropriate Japanese prints. In this way one can bring into our homes a suggestion of that charming custom of the Japanese by which a flower or a picture or both hold for a brief time the place of honor in the living-room, generally with a suggestion of the spirit of the season in the outer world."

Wall pockets were produced in volume during the 1920s and 1930s. They decorated Jazz Age and Depression era walls with a bit of greenery tumbling

from them. While many collectors concentrate on pockets from this era, wall pockets seem to have been produced more or less continuously from the early part of the century to the present.

Several items should be mentioned that are sometimes confused with wall pockets by the new collector.

A popular ceramic object of the twenties and thirties that sometimes hung on the wall were toothbrush holders. These fanciful objects were commonly produced in Japan and often have the same lusters and glazes seen in Japanese pockets. These are sometimes depicted as people (although other characters were used) with two to four square holes where the toothbrushes were inserted. There may also be a small concave shelf at the bottom on which to lay the tube of toothpaste (See PLATE 8).

Occasionally you may run across what looks like a wall pocket made of chalk or plaster of Paris. Although there may be a small indention at the top, there will obviously not be enough room or depth for flowers. These objects were sometimes used as early room deoderizers or fresheners. Perfume was poured into the indention where it was obsorbed into the porous body. The smell of the perfume was then released into the

*PLATE 7. This fancy, cornucopia-shaped wall pocket probably held a bouquet of dried flowers. Drying and arranging flowers for winter decoration was a popular woman's pastime during the Victorian era.*

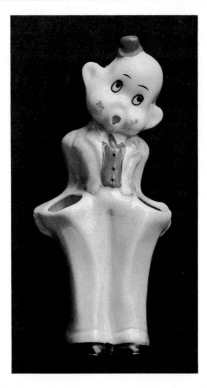

*PLATE 8. This 6¾" luster, toothbrush holder was imported from Japan during the 1920s. There is room for a toothbrush in each of his outstretched pockets. Such toothbrush holders are eagerly sought by collectors.*

# Marks

The United States passed a law in 1891 requiring that all imported ceramics bear the name of the country of origin. This law was amended in 1914 to include the phrase "Made in . . ." as part of the mark. While this may help you narrow down your study of wall pockets, you should not assume the piece was made prior to 1891 just because it is unmarked. American-made pockets did not have to be marked and many pockets also had paper labels that have long since fallen off.

In collecting certain types of ceramics, marked pieces are much more valuable than unmarked pieces. Wall pocket collectors need not be so selective. Once in a great while, someone may try to justify a price on a Japanese pocket based on its mark. In general, marks should not be of much concern for collectors. Exceptions include collecting a pocket of a certain type of pottery or porcelain such as Roseville or Noritake. In that case, the buyer should use the standards set for that particular type.

It should also be noted that many American-made wall pockets and other ceramics were marked USA during World War II. It was considered a sign of patriotism for a company to mark its wares in that way during the war. Some collectors think that the USA mark denotes one manufacturer such as McCoy or Shawnee. That is not always the case and can lead to misidentification. It was also necessary to mark wares USA if they were to be exported.

room over time. A more practical application for these objects might have also been as match safes (PLATE 9).

String holders are sometimes confused with wall pockets. Before the invention of scotch tape, string was an important item to keep handy in the home. String holders shaped like human or animal faces with a small hole in the mouth and a hollow back large enough to hold a ball of string were hung on the kitchen wall. The string hung through the hole in the mouth ready to be pulled out and used (See PLATE 10).

Fine cars of the twenties and thirties were sometimes appointed with bud vases that hung either on the post between the front and back seat or behind the back seat. These bud vases were held in a metal rack that was attached to the car. The vases were generally made of clear or colored glass. Carnival glass bud vases were also produced. These car vases generally are not found with a hole in the back for hanging from a nail as wall pockets are. While car bud vases were not originally designed for use in the home as wall pockets were, they are nevertheless an interesting addition to a wall pocket collection, particularly if one specializes in glass pockets ( See PLATE 11).

*PLATE 9. This small, plaster face is only 3" tall. She held either matches or scent.*

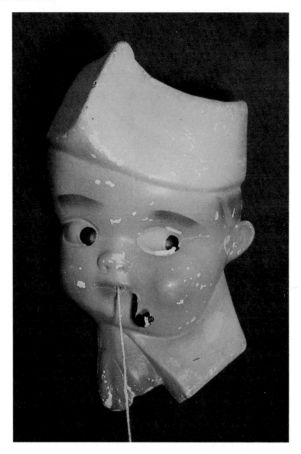

PLATE 10. String holders such as this one are popular collectibles. The flaking paint on this one probably diminishes its value. String holders were rendered obsolete by the invention of adhesive tape.

PLATE 11. This is a typical car bud vase. These were sold to stores by glass manufacturers which suggests that bud vases were added to cars by their owners rather than at the automobile factory. This bud vase was priced at about $75.00 by the dealer.

PLATE 12. Notice how the blue luster on this Japanese pocket is worn down to the white porcelain body on the bottom of the pocket.

## Condition and Value

A good general rule for buying wall pockets is that as condition declines so should the price. Keep in mind that wall pockets received little heavy use. They were decorative objects that were rarely handled. Therefore, unless you know the pocket is extremely unusual, buy only those in mint condition.

The most common damage to wall pockets (aside from falling off the wall) is from water. Some pockets are crazed and stained from water left in them, sometimes for years. Original owners displayed cut flowers or grew ivy in wall pockets. When you examine the insides of many pockets, you will find mineral deposits left by years of standing water from which ivy probably grew. It is a tribute to many wall pocket manufacturers that these pockets are unstained and show no crazing on the outside. Stay away from very damaged pieces, but pockets with mineral deposits are acceptable if the body and glaze are undamaged.

Luster is a very low fire glazed finish and easily scratched and worn. If a lustered pocket appears as if the luster has been partially rubbed off, pass it up. Note that at the bottom of PLATE 12, the blue luster is almost worn down to the white porcelain base.

Production flaws are generally not acceptable. Cracks, someone's fingerprints immortalized in the glaze, or poor hand painting reduce the quality of a piece as much as accidental damage.

Wall pockets are rarely one-of-a-kind objects. The Japanese ones particularly were imported in volume. Therefore, look for good glaze colors, good painting technique, and luster (if it has it) in excellent condition.

## Prices

As stated in the introduction, wall pockets are inexpensive collectibles that are not difficult to find. Nevertheless, prices vary widely. The same pocket may be $5.00 at a garage sale, $12.50 at a flea market, $25.00 in an antique mall, and $45.00 in an upscale antique shop. The dilemma for the collector then becomes, "how much is my time worth?" If you enjoy getting up early on Friday and Saturday morning and driving to multiple garage sales, then eventually you will come up with some bargains. The key word in that last sentence, however, is "eventually." The same may be said for flea markets, although the proportion of junk to treasure is more in favor of treasure. In other words, part of what you pay for in an antique shop is the time the shop owner spent finding the items in the shop.

The collector must weigh her time against discretionary income in deciding how much she is willing to pay and where she is going to shop. Even individuals with limited resources should not rule out shops, however. Dealers are almost always willing to share their knowledge with novice collectors and bargains can be found anywhere.

Here are some general rules for prices.

1. Mint condition is worth more than damage.
2. Rare pieces are worth more than common ones.
3. Intricate design and shape increases value.
4. Unusual size increases value — either unusually large or unusually small pieces.
5. Designs that are currently popular (i.e. Deco) are generally more expensive.
6. Pairs may be worth more than one of the pair times two. This is particularly true if it is matched, but nonidentical pair, as with a male and female or mirror image pairs.
7. As with all antiques and collectibles, buy the best that you can afford.
8. Know something about the general field of ceramics. As mentioned earlier, some Japanese pockets are being described and priced as majolica, an expensive collectible produced in Europe and America. Don't pay for something you are not getting.

## Caring for Your Collection

The best way to avoid having your pockets broken is to hang them where they won't get knocked off. If you hang them on a wall behind a sofa, make sure they are hung high enough that persons sitting on the sofa won't hit them with their heads or hands. If they are hung in a hallway, be sure the hall is wide enough that people won't bump them with their shoulders.

Walls that vibrate create problems for wall pockets. Window air conditioning units create considerable vibration as do washers and dryers that back up to a wall. Slamming doors may do the same thing. Over time, your pockets may gradually vibrate off their nails and fall off the wall. To avoid this, use long thin brads driven into the wall at a sharp angle. Check your pockets occasionally and push them back flush against the wall.

Like any other ceramic, wall pockets need an occasional washing. Avoid soaking the pockets in water for long periods for the same reason you would not leave water in them. Sponge them off with a mild soap and water and give them a quick rinse. Don't use extremely hot water and don't put them in the dishwasher. Dry them with a soft cloth and avoid drying them with paper towels. Paper towels contain microscopic pieces of wood that can scratch the glaze or luster on your pocket.

Buy yourself a set of felt tip pens in a variety of colors. You may be able to camouflage a small chip or glaze imperfection with them.

Do not use abrasive cleaners on your pockets. Luster will scratch easily as will some other low fire glazes.

Occasionally paint rather than glaze may be used on a pocket as an accent. This technique is called cold painting. Since it is not fired on, you risk washing or scratching it off with an abrasive cleaner.

Avoid using ammonia or ammonia based cleaners on pieces that are decorated with gold and silver. Many glass cleaners use ammonia as a primary ingredient. A mixture of water and white vinegar does an excellent job of cleaning glass or ceramic surfaces.

An early process to impart luster on carnival glass was sensitive to the effects of sunlight. If you are uncertain as to the method used on a lustered glass pocket, do not place it in direct sunlight. One expert on carnival glass recommends that it only be displayed under florescent light.

As a general rule, do not display colored glass in the direct rays of the sun. The pocket may become discolored.

## Cataloging Your Collection

The casual collector may not care to do this but some collectors use price stickers on the back of their pockets to record how much they paid for the pocket and the date of acquisition.

A somewhat more romantic, fun version helps collectors remember where they were and who they were with. In addition to the price and date, they write a brief note about the circumstances of the purchase. Many people collect while on vacation or weekend jaunts and their pockets become a souvenir of their experiences. The note helps them remember those

events. The note is tucked into the pocket for future reference. Collecting is a pleasant, refreshing experience that takes you away from your daily schedule. Every brief, ten minute run through of an out-of-the-way shop is a little adventure. Keeping notes on your purchases helps you relive those adventures. More pragmatically, these notes also give you a record of where you tend to find your collectibles so that if you want to become more systematic, you know where you should concentrate your time and effort.

Some collectors like to have a photographic record of their collection. Photos are helpful if you want to sell or trade with other collectors. They are also very important if you own expensive wall pockets or have a very extensive collection. In case of fire or theft, a photo would be important in dealing with an insurance company. Needless to say, photos for insurance should be stored somewhere besides your house or else in a fireproof safe in your home.

Many collectors submitted pictures of their wall pockets for inclusion in this book. Most had not tried to photograph their pockets before and found it to be more challenging than they had anticipated.

While I am not a professional photographer by any means, I would like to make some suggestions for producing a photographic record of your collection.

Use a good, 35 mm, single lens reflex camera. I used a 20-year-old Canon AE1 with a 50 mm lens. This is a good, all-purpose lens that came with the camera. A camera such as this will allow you to focus to within three feet of an object and it is important to get as close as possible in order to capture detail. Lenses on this type of camera screw on and off and it would be possible to buy a lens that would focus even closer than the 50 mm allows. Adapters that are basically magnifiers are also available that screw directly on to the 50 mm lens and allow you to focus even closer.

A "point and shoot" camera is not a good choice for this type of photography for two reasons. Most easy-to-use cameras have a fixed focus that does not allow you to focus closer than about five feet. This is too far away for detailed shots. If you attempt to get any closer, the photo will be out of focus. Also, there is often a difference in size between what you see in the view finder and what you ultimately see in the picture. The objects in the finished picture will be somewhat smaller than what your eye sees in the view finder. This is not the case with single lens reflex cameras. The size you see in the view finder is exactly what the photo will look like.

I used 100 ISO film which gives very good color definition to photos. Fast film, such as 400 ISO, requires less light but is better suited for capturing movement. Since your pockets aren't going anywhere, it is better to supply more light and use 100 ISO film. It is possible to buy even slower film such as 50 or 25 ISO. Their use, however, will probably necessitate the use of a tripod and that makes your picture taking more complicated. Kodak and Fuji both make very good quality film and paper. I wouldn't take a chance on off-brands of film.

If at all possible, work outside on a clear day. Avoid using a flash if possible. A flash creates a glare on shiny surfaces and often leaves the pocket looking over exposed. I got good pictures working in open, even shade. If you must work inside, use as much artificial light as possible. I went to the local discount store and bought two silvery, clamp-on utility lights with 100 watt bulbs as extra lighting. I clamped the lights on chairs or had someone hold them. This gave a light source on either side of the pocket to be photographed. I sometimes taped a thin, white cloth over the light for a more even, diffuse light. Using artificial, incandescent light creates something of a problem for indoor photography. The film found hanging at the check out stand that most of us buy is really designed for natural sunlight. When used with incandescent light, it tends to have a yellow tint since the light does not supply all the color wave lengths that sunlight does. A good developer will compensate for that by adding a color filter when developing your film that will eliminate the yellow. However, if you are a real purist, you might want to consider using tungsten film which is designed to correct this yellowing effect in incandescent light.

Of course, you can photograph the wall pocket on a wall if the wall provides a nice, even background and the light is good. However, you will get equally nice pictures by laying your pockets on a flat surface and shooting down at them. I used a dark background such as a piece of burgundy velvet, but lighter backgrounds work well too. If you use an automatic camera that adjusts for light, a white background will sometimes "fool" the camera because of the light it reflects. The camera adjusts for the light reflected by the background rather than the wall pocket and the result is that the pocket may end up looking dark and underexposed. I often used the floor or a chair seat as my surface with my background fabric laid over it.

Good quality color is important in this type of photo and where you have your film developed can make a big difference. Sometimes drugstore developing works out fine but I pay more and have my film developed at a specialty photo store.

## Pictures and Prices

The pockets represented in this book are from private collections or the stock of dealers in malls or shops. Many hundreds of wall pockets have been produced over the years. They are still being produced. It would be impossible to show them all. Pockets pictured in this book have been selected to give the reader an idea of different types available as well as what is common and what is unusual.

The prices are based on what the pocket might cost in a shop or antique show. A general range is given rather than a set price to give collectors a general idea of what they might pay. These prices are not meant to be used by dealers to set prices or by a buyer to determine a bargaining price. Remember that prices vary depending on whether you are at a garage sale, a flea market, or in a shop. Antique and collectible prices seem to be higher on either coast than they are in the middle of the country. Therefore, you will probably pay more in New York City than you will in Peoria.

## Pocket Producers

Wall pockets have been produced by many pottery and porcelain makers over the years. They can be found in the popular blue willow pattern, in majolica, Japanese lusterware, and many other sought after patterns and styles. Hummels have been produced as pockets. Most of the well-known American arts and crafts potteries produced wall pockets as part of their decorative lines. A recent price guide listed over 85 different companies and style groups with wall pockets as part of their line.

If you buy a marked wall pocket, you might start your investigation of it by looking up the maker in a general price guide.

# American Manufacturers

Some of the earliest pottery wall pockets made in America were crafted in the Shenandoah Valley, according to Rena London, in a 1979 article in the *Antique Trader Weekly.* Various potters who worked in that area produced pockets to hold flowers and matches. These pockets were decorated with birds and flowers in high relief, according to Ms. London. In Ohio, many farmers learned that their clay earth which was so difficult for plowing, was ideal for making utilitarian wares needed for a farm. By 1840, ninety-nine potteries were listed as businesses in Ohio.

In the late 1800s and shortly after the turn of the century, many potteries were formed that would later produce many beautiful ceramic wares. Zanesville, Ohio, possessed a fortuitous combination of good clay for potting and abundant natural gas to fire kilns. Zanesville became known as the "Clay City." Several famous American wall pocket manufacturers, Weller, Roseville, McCoy, and Hull, were located in this area. These potteries all produced many exquisite wall pockets. One could have a large collection of wall pockets by just specializing in one of these makers.

During the early years of pottery production in this area of the country, talented artists were recruited from all over the world to work in this budding industry. Some were responsible for creating or executing designs while others created unique glazes. These craftsmen and craftswomen would often work for one pottery then go to work for another or form potteries of their own. As a result, examination of the works of these potteries, especially during the first twenty years of this century, reveals marked similarities among the lines produced by each company.

One invention that had a profound influence on the pottery production of this country was the airbrush. The airbrush was patented in 1884, by Laura Fry, who first worked for Rookwood. It allowed for the smooth application of glazes to the clay body and for the gentle color shading that characterizes so much of the American art pottery from the early part of the twentieth century. Ms. Fry left Rookwood and went to work

for the company that would later become Weller.

While the famous potteries of Ohio began by producing truly one-of-a-kind art pottery, most gradually turned to mass-produced wares. These lines still retained a certain art pottery look but could be decorated by relatively unskilled laborers rather than the artist who did the original design. Most wares were in low relief and were decorated with airbrushes or sponges, following the embossed lines left by the mold. These pieces generally had a floral theme.

It is interesting to note that during the early years of pottery making, much of the hand decoration of production wares was done by women. Before the advent of child labor laws, many of these women were merely young girls who worked to help support their families rather than attend school. In the post-Victorian society of the early 1900s, females were considered particularly well suited to the sort of detailed work that was required in decorating. Despite the importance of women in this industry, most of the famous designers were men. This fact probably also reflects the collective mind set of the times.

World War II played an important role in the development of American potteries. The war in Europe had already disrupted ceramic production in most of the European countries and imports were at a virtual standstill. The bombing of Pearl Harbor brought and end to the import of Japanese ceramics into the United States eliminating an important competitor. Also, because ceramics had little strategic importance for the war, potteries could continue to produce their wares and did not have to allocate their factories to the war effort. One reported exception was the Nelson McCoy Company which produced a ceramic land mine for the United States Armed Forces. This ceramic land mine supposedly had the advantage of being more difficult to detect by the enemy than traditional metal land mines. Unimpeded by foreign competition, American potteries flourished in the artificial, protected economic environment provided by the war.

If the war was a boon for American potteries, the

end of the war had an equally detrimental effect on them. The Japanese industry roared back into production, flooding the market with cheap ceramic wares, often direct imitations of American products. With their higher labor costs, it became increasingly difficult for American potteries to compete against their foreign rivals. In addition to fierce competition and higher labor costs, the fickle tastes of the American public also contributed to the demise of the large potteries. Most tried to alter their products to meet these changing tastes of the American consumer but all were ultimately unsuccessful. The introduction of plastic as a household product hurt those potteries that had also produced kitchen, restaurant, and hotel wares. One by one, the great American producers of hand-decorated pottery went out of business.

# Weller

The Weller Pottery Company was created in Ohio, in 1872, when Samuel Weller began producing utilitarian wares from the clay found on his farm. Ten years later he purchased his first building in Zanesville and began the sophisticated family pottery business that would exist until 1948.

Before the turn of the century, Weller produced beautiful art pottery and by 1902 had practically cornered the market on mass-produced art pottery. Weller would take young men and women and teach them to paint one thing, such as flowers, scenery, or portraits, and pay them low wages for their work. They turned out many beautiful pieces originally designed by a well paid artist. A reporter who visited Weller's plant in 1902 was not allowed to visit the design department to prevent the spread of designs or glaze formulae to competitors.

Until 1900, Weller produced many large pieces of ceramics. It was very stylish to have a jardiniere and pedestal as well as an umbrella holder in the entry hall of the Victorian home. The turn of the century brought a subtle shift of popular taste away from these monumental pieces and toward smaller decorative items, including wall pockets.

The turn of the century also brought another change that impacted the large scale production of shaped and molded wall pockets. Weller shifted from the use of potter's wheels to the use of plaster of Paris molds. Pots thrown on a wheel were always smooth and symmetrical. While decorations could be replicated, each piece was basically a one-of-a-kind item. With plaster molds, it was possible to reproduce a shape again and again. Wall pockets could be produced by flattening a wheel-thrown piece on one side but molds allowed for a variety of asymmetrical shapes and sizes.

Wall pockets appear to have been a standard item in Weller lines throughout the history of the pottery. Wall pockets appeared as a part of all of Weller's best lines. These lines included Arcola, Ardsley, Art Nouveau, Blue Drapery, Cloudburst, Fairfield, Florala, Fruitone, Glendale, Green Orris, Hudson, Ivory, Klyro, Knifewood, Lavonia, Lorbeek, Malverne, Marvo, Oak Leaf, Parian, Pearl, Pumila, Roma, Sabrinian, Selma, Sivertone, Woodcraft, Woodrose, and Zona. Wall pockets were also made in Weller's novelty lines. Weller pockets had rich, colorful glazes and detailed modeling. It was not unusual for a design line to have several different wall pockets in it. Roma, a line characterized by a cream background with fruit and flower decorations, was popular and included several different wall pockets. The Woodcraft line had many unusual wall pockets decorated with birds or woodland animals.

Over the years Weller used a wide variety of marks on its wares. Generally the mark included the name Weller although there are a few exceptions. Some marks were die impressed into the bottom, some were incised, and ink stamp marks were also used. Block print, die impressed marks are generally from Weller's middle period (after 1910) and later marks were script signatures in the mold. Some pieces were also unmarked.

Weller pockets were beautifully crafted and have a distinctive art pottery look. Even in the later years of the company when they were struggling to survive with mass-produced lines, their wares retained a high standard of designs and glazes. The Weller company was particularly hurt by the influx of Japanese imports throughout its history. Line for line copies of Weller pockets can be found that were made in Japan. These can be distinguished not only by their marks but also by the use of glazes not seen on authentic Weller wares.

Weller pockets are now quite expensive by most wall pocket standards.

*PLATE 13 (left). Weller Roma. Height 8". Mark: impressed Weller. Production of Roma began in 1914. The Roma line is characterized by a cream background glaze with red, blue, and green floral and fruit decorations. Estimated value: $95.00 to $125.00*

*PLATE 14 (right). Weller Marvo. Height 9". Unmarked. Production began on the Marvo line in the late 1920s. This line was characterized by molded, raised foliage of palms and ferns. It came in four colors, green as pictured, rust, blue, and mauve. Estimated value: $95.00 to $120.00.*

*PLATE 15. Weller Woodrose. Height 7". Mark: 348. Woodrose production began around 1925. The Woodrose line had more than one wall pocket, but the line is characterized by an oak bucket shape that was designed by Rudolph Lorber. Estimated value: $75.00 to $95.00.*

*PLATE 16. Weller Woodrose. Height 5¾". Mark: impressed Weller. This is a smaller, more slender version of PLATE 15. Both of these pockets are in standard Woodrose glaze colors. Woodrose pockets in these glaze colors are relatively common as Weller pockets go. Estimated value: $75.00 to $95.00.*

PLATE 17. Weller Woodrose. Height 7". Mark: impressed Weller. This is the same shape as PLATE 16 but 1¼" taller. This pocket is remarkable for its atypical periwinkle blue background glaze color. Dealer price: $98.00.

PLATE 18. Weller Woodcraft. Height 8". Unmarked. This line first appeared in 1917. Weller made a wide variety of elaborate wall pockets in the Woodcraft line. Predominate glaze colors were brown and dark green in keeping with the rustic theme. Flowers, birds, and animals were glazed in appropriate but subdued colors. Some Woodcraft pockets were very elaborate. These pockets often included birds or squirrels perched on a limb or coming out of a hole in the pocket. Estimated value: $95.00 to $125.00.

PLATE 19. Weller Selma. Height 7". Mark: impressed Weller. This shiny glaze is somewhat unusual for Weller. There is apparently some confusion about this line as it is sometimes referred to as Knifewood. Estimated value: $75.00 to $95.00.

PLATE 21. This picture illustrates the variety of sizes and shapes of wall pockets available in the Weller Roma and Roma Dupont line. Roma was a popular Weller line designed by Rudolph Lorber in 1914. Roma may be the most plentiful of all the Weller lines.

PLATE 20. Weller Roma Dupont. Height 11". Mark: impressed Weller. The Dupont line was introduced in 1915. There appeared to be some overlap between Roma and Dupont and the Huxfords identify this particular pocket as Roma Dupont. Estimated value: $125.00 to $150.00.

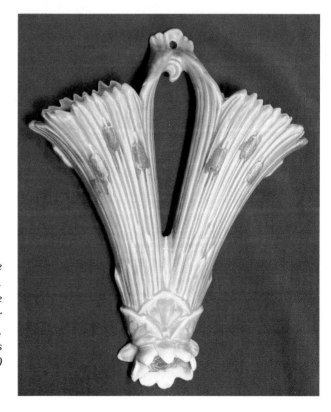

PLATE 22. Weller Ardsley double mouth wall pocket. Height 11½". Mark: ink stamped Weller Ware. The Ardsley line was introduced by Weller in the early to mid-1920s. Cattails, iris, and lily pads are design themes of this line. Estimated value: $125.00 to $150.00.

PLATE 24. Weller Roma wall pocket. Height 7". Mark: impressed Weller. This is another design variation on the popular Roma line. Estimated value: $95.00 to $120.00.

PLATE 23. Weller Green Orris wall pocket. Height approximately 8". Unmarked. Green Orris is something of a departure from Weller's usual lines. It is generally unmarked and a red clay was used rather than the usual light colored one. Over this red body, a matte green glaze was applied and when fired, the red showed through. This line was quite similar to the one called Moss Aztec by the Peters and Reed Pottery. Estimated value: $125.00 to $150.00.

PLATE 25. Weller Klyro. Height 7¾". Unmarked. The Klyro line was produced beginning in 1928. It is characterized by a reticulated design at the top. Estimated value: $95.00 to $120.00.

PLATE 26. Early hand inscribed Weller mark.

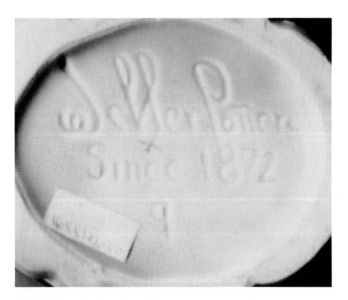

PLATE 27. Weller in-mold script mark. Weller's wares may be marked with a variety of ink stamps, die stamps, paper labels, or hand incised marks. After 1935, however, this in-mold, script mark was most often used.

PLATE 28. Weller die impressed mark. A small, block-printed Weller mark was used before 1910. The larger size of the mark indicates that it was produced after that date.

# Roseville

The Roseville Pottery Company was established in Roseville, Ohio, in 1892, and later moved to Zanesville, Ohio. Throughout its history, the Roseville Pottery Company produced high quality wares of considerable artistic merit. The Roseville Pottery Company, like most of the American potteries of its time, began by producing true, individually created art pottery. However, not far into the twentieth century, Roseville turned to the mass production of what could more accurately be described as commercial art wares. The originals were designed by artists and then plaster of Paris molds were made of them and slip cast in mass. Most of the designs could then be decorated by trained employees. The decorations generally did not require a high degree of artistic ability which kept overall labor costs down.

Generally, Roseville pottery was produced in a soft, satin matte glaze. Some of the early art pottery was produced in gloss glazes but shiny glazes did not reappear in any number until much later. The pottery, struggling to maintain its market in the fifties, introduced several lines with shiny glazes in a vain attempt to recapture the imagination of the fickle American consumer.

Many of the wall pockets made by Roseville were produced during the middle periods and later, although Chloron, introduced in 1907, included at least nine different wall pockets. The middle period extended from about 1915 to the mid-1930s. Wall pockets were also produced in the floral lines of the later years of the company. Lines with wall pockets included Blackberry, Bleeding Heart, Burmese, Bushberry, Carnelian II, Ceramic Design, Chloron, Clematis, Corinthian, Cosmos, Dahlrose, Dogwood I and II, Donatello, Earlam, Ferella, Florentine, Freesia, Gardenia, Imperial II, Jonquil, La Rose, Lombardy, Lotus, Matt Green, Mayfair, Morning Glory, Moss, Orian, Panel, Peony, Pine Cone, Poppy, Rosecraft, Rozane, Savona, Silhouette, Sunflower, Thornapple, Velmoss Scroll, Vista, and White Rose. This list may not be complete but should give the reader some idea of the number of wall pockets produced by this company. Most of these lines had more than one style of wall pockets and each style might come in more than one color combination.

Roseville used a variety of marks including an ink stamp mark and marks modeled into the mold. To present a challenge to the collector, some Roseville is unmarked.

Like Weller pockets, Roseville wall pockets tend to be quite expensive. However, their beauty and consistently high craftsmanship make them well worth the money.

*PLATE 29. Roseville Apple Blossom. Height 8". Mark: Roseville molded in relief. Production of this pattern began in 1948. Estimated value: $125.00 to $150.00.*

PLATE 30. Roseville Freesia. Height 8½". Mark: Roseville, #366-8 molded in relief. Production began in 1945. Estimated value: $125.00 to $150.00.

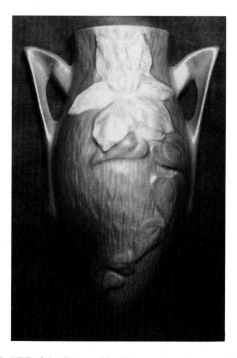

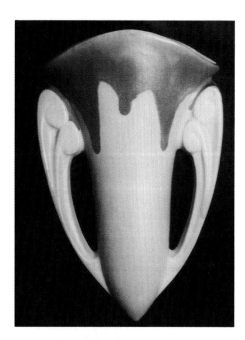

PLATE 31. Roseville Clematis. Height 8½". Mark: Roseville, #1295-8 molded in relief. Production began in 1944. Estimated value: $125.00 to $150.00.

PLATE 32. Roseville Carnelian I. Height 8". Mark: Rv ink stamp. Production began in the early 1900s. Estimated value: $95.00 to $135.00.

PLATE 33. Roseville Corinthian. Height 8". Mark: Rv ink stamp. Production began in 1923. Estimated value: $95.00 to $135.00.

PLATE 34. Roseville La Rosa. Height 7½". Mark: Rv ink stamp. Production began in 1924. Estimated value: $125.00 to $150.00.

PLATE 35. Roseville Rosecraft Panel. Height 9½". Mark: Rv ink stamp. Panel was first produced in 1920. Estimated value: $125.00 to $150.00.

*PLATE 37. Roseville Yellow Tint. Height 12".*
*Unmarked. This deco styled pocket is covered in a cream*
*colored matte glaze. Where the glaze pooled in the deco-*
*ration, it has a yellow tint. Dealer price: $248.00.*

*PLATE 36. Roseville Rosecraft Panel. Height 9½". Mark:*
*Rv ink stamp. This is a slightly different coloration than*
*PLATE 35 with more overall brown tones. Dealer price:*
*$279.00. The price of Roseville wall pockets has been*
*rising rapidly and at antique shows is often higher than*
*the price guides.*

*PLATE 38. Roseville Cosmos. Height 8". Mark: incised*
*in script, Roseville USA 1286-8. These wall pockets were*
*also identified with foil paper labels which might be miss-*
*ing from current examples. Production on this lovely*
*wall pocket began around 1940. It was produced with a*
*blue and green background in addition to the tan back-*
*ground shown. The double mouth on this pocket is*
*unusual and desirable. Antique show price: $298.00.*

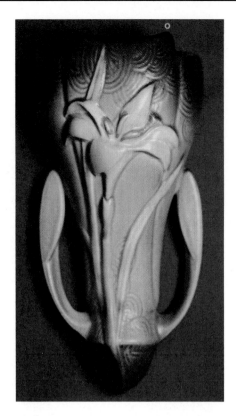

PLATE 39. *Roseville Zephyr Lily. Height 8". Mark: mold-ed* Roseville USA 1297-8. *The background color shown was called Evergreen. This pocket could also be found in background colors of Burmuda Blue and Sienna Tan. Production on this line began in the 1940s. Antique show price: $190.00.*

PLATE 40. *Roseville Silhouette. Height 8". Mark: mold-ed* Roseville USA 766-8. *This line was introduced in 1952. Roseville identified this color as turquoise. Antique show price: $225.00.*

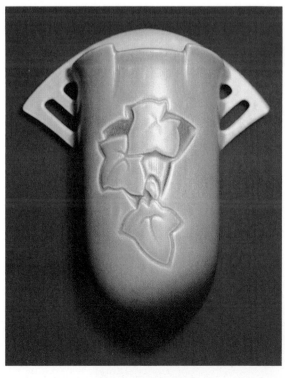

PLATE 41. *Roseville Silhouette. Height 8". Mark: molded* Roseville USA 766-8. *This rather orangy-brown color was called tan by the company. In addition to turquoise and tan, a Silhouette wall pocket was also produced in rose and white with turquoise highlights. Estimated value: $175.00 to $200.00.*

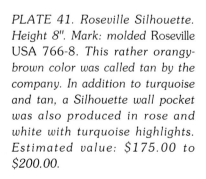

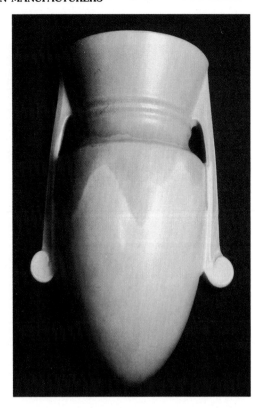

PLATE 42. Roseville Carnelian I. Height 9½".
Mark: Rv ink stamp. This is an early Roseville
line which was introduced between 1910 and
1915. Antique show price: $179.00.

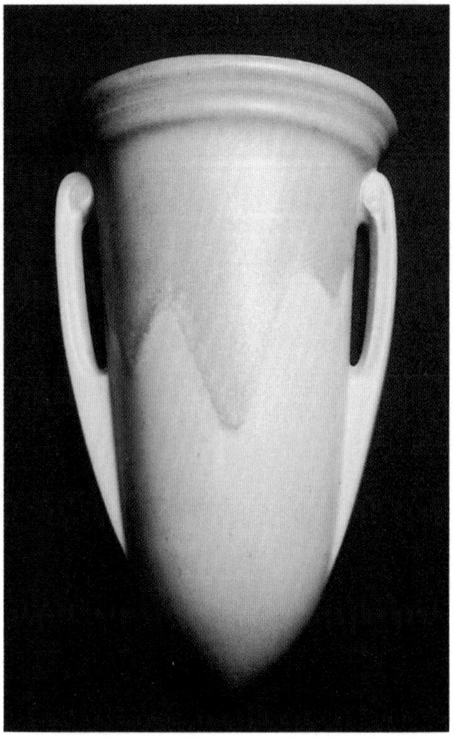

PLATE 43. Roseville Carnelian II. Height
8". Unmarked. The second Carnelian line
was introduced around 1915. The pockets in this line have classical urn shapes
and have a lighter matte, background
color and a darker glaze that runs down
from the rim. Estimated value: $125.00
to $150.00.

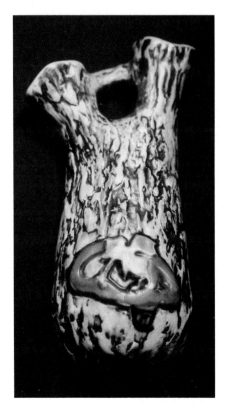

PLATE 44. Roseville Imperial
I. Height 10". Unmarked. This
is another older line that was
first offered in 1916. Imperial I
had a rustic, organic look that
this double mouth pocket
exemplifies. Antique show
price: $279.00.

PLATE 45. *Roseville Windridge. Height approximately 7". Mark: molded Roseville 266-4. The shiny glaze and style of this pocket suggests that this is one of Roseville's later design lines. This pocket was made in other glaze colors. Estimated value: $90.00.*

PLATE 46. *Roseville Mayfair. Height 8". Mark: Roseville USA 1014-8. This pocket is of a very rare design that fits into a corner. It was produced in several glaze colors. The color shown was known as "greige" because it appears to be a cross between beige and gray. Estimated value: $150.00 to $170.00.*

PLATE 47. *This is an example of a Roseville ink stamp mark. This mark is found on older Roseville pieces.*

PLATE 48. *This is an example of a later mark that was part of the mold and appears raised on the pieces.*

# McCoy

McCoy potters worked around Roseville, Ohio, in the late 1880s. The Nelson McCoy Sanitary Stoneware Company was established in 1910. This firm became known as the Nelson McCoy Pottery Company in 1933. When they expanded their factory in 1940, they began to produce the novelty art ware for which they became famous. During that same time, they also produced ceramic land mines for the U.S. government for use in World War II. Both lines were no doubt real attention getters!

McCoy was a prolific producer of wall pockets with over 25 designs. During the 1940s they helped fill the gap left when Japanese wall pockets ceased to be imported.

The McCoy company used over a dozen marks during its existence. Most incorporate the name McCoy in the mark although some early pieces were marked NM USA (the NM stood for Nelson McCoy). Unfortunately for the wall pocket collector, many McCoy pockets are also unmarked.

Some wall pockets had a combination of glaze and cold paint decoration. Others have only glaze. McCoy pockets often have decorations applied to the main body of the pocket such as a bird applied to a birdbath or a flower. These three-dimensional objects required hand application and extra time to execute. Many times, McCoy pockets are found with these decorations chipped or totally broken off.

McCoy wall pockets can be difficult to find. They are still more moderately priced than some other American pockets such as Weller and Roseville. Nevertheless, McCoy collectors report that wall pockets in this line are becoming more and more expensive. There are collectors who only collect McCoy pockets in their many variations. These collectors often buy and sell their pockets through the want ads of *McCoy Matters*, a newsletter about McCoy. Others have more luck finding them in Ohio, where they were originally produced. It is still possible to find McCoy pockets in antique malls and flea markets from time to time.

*PLATE 49. The McCoy pear (left) and orange (right) wall pockets. Height of both 7" x 6" wide. These pockets are sometimes found with quality control letter marks on them such as the letters L or R. The pear colors are glaze but the orange is cold painted. If this pocket is found with the orange paint washed off, it may be identified as a lemon. McCoy did not make a lemon wall pocket. Estimated value: $35.00. The orange may be found as low as $18.00.*

*PLATE 50. McCoy banana (left) and apple (right). Height of both 7" x 6" wide. Note the slightly different green glaze color on the two pockets. It was not unusual for McCoy glaze colors to vary from batch to batch. An unusual variation in the fruit pocket series is brown leaves rather than green ones. The apple pocket and pear pocket have been seen with brown leaves. Estimated value: Apple $35.00. Banana $35.00 to $75.00.*

*PLATE 51. Two of three grape wall pocket variations. Height of both 7" x 6" wide. The pocket on the left is known as a red grape wall pocket and the one on the right is the purple grape pocket. Estimated value: $35.00 each.*

*PLATE 52. On the right is the white grape pocket by McCoy. It is considered to be somewhat rare. On the left is the back of the banana wall pocket, shown because it is typical of the backs of all of the McCoy fruit pockets. None have the McCoy name in the mark. McCoy began the manufacture of the fruit pockets in 1953. Estimated value: white grape $75.00 with slight, no see damage to $175.00 for perfect.*

PLATE 53. McCoy Easter lily wall pocket. Height 7½". Mark: McCoy, Made in USA. McCoy began production of this pocket in 1948. The one shown is in white but it was also produced in yellow. These pockets are seen occasionally. Estimated value: $35.00 to $45.00.

PLATE 54. McCoy little clown wall pocket. Height 8½". The wall pocket is shown in the standard paint colors in which it was produced. The cold paint washes off easily. This pocket was first produced in 1943. Estimated value: $40.00 to $50.00.

PLATE 55. McCoy bird on birdbath wall pocket. Height 8". Mark: McCoy. Pictured in aqua with a yellow bird, this pocket was also made with a yellow birdbath with a green bird. Production began on the pocket in 1949. This pocket is seen occasionally but often the bird is damaged or broken off. Estimated value: $40.00 to $50.00.

PLATE 56. McCoy cuckoo clock. Height 8" not counting the clock weights. This pocket was first produced in 1952 and came in a variety of colors as well as either Roman or Arabic numerals. Pocket pictured is pink with a blue bird and Arabic numerals, trimmed in gold. Note that the clock weights are hollow. This pocket was also produced in brown and ivory with a green bird and Roman numerals, blue and ivory with an aqua bird and Roman numerals or Arabic numerals, pink with a blue bird and Roman numerals without the gold trim, green and brown with a yellow bird and Roman or Arabic numerals. The cuckoo clock in all of its variations is considered a rare wall pocket, especially in perfect condition. Estimated value: $45.00 to $60.00.

PLATE 57. McCoy cornucopia. Height 9½". This unmarked pocket was first produced in the mid to late 1970s. The flowers on this pocket are decals and it was produced with a variety of decals. This pocket was also produced decorated with an overall design of blue sponged on a white background. Estimated value: $18.00 to $30.00.

PLATE 58. *This picture of a McCoy collection shows a variety of McCoy cuckoo clocks and large cornucopias.*

PLATE 59. *McCoy produced a variety of wall pockets with objects superimposed on a trivet. Pictured on the right is the most easily found of this series, an iron on a trivet. All of the trivet wall pockets are 8" high by 6" wide and are marked McCoy USA as shown in the picture on the left. In addition to the color combination shown, the iron on a trivet also came with a gray iron on a black trivet, a yellow iron on a black or gray trivet, and a black iron on a lime green trivet. The wall pocket in the picture shows some remnants of cold painting that has been washed away. Estimated value: $45.00 to $60.00.*

PLATE 60. *McCoy owls on a trivet. Height 8". Mark: McCoy USA. This pocket is only known to have been produced in the color combination shown of brown birds with cold painted eyes and toes on a yellow trivet. Estimated value: $45.00 to $60.00.*

PLATE 61. *McCoy lovebirds on a trivet. Height 8". Mark: McCoy USA. This is the only color combination known for this pocket although the birds are sometimes seen with more pronounced brown shading than is pictured. Estimated value: $45.00 to $60.00.*

PLATE 62. McCoy Mexican man. Height 7". Unmarked. Pictured is the back of a yellow version and the front of an aqua version of a man holding a sombrero. A rare version of this pocket is black glaze with cold painted accents. Another rare variation is of the man holding a book rather than a hat. Manufactured first in 1941. Estimated value: for more common yellow or aqua $25.00 to $40.00.

PLATE 63. McCoy small, one handled lily. Height 6". Mark: stylized NM, USA, 1940-43. In addition to the aqua color shown, it was also produced in yellow, white, and lavender. This wall pocket is rarely seen on the market. Estimated value: $15.00 to $35.00.

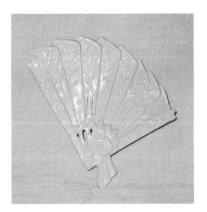

PLATE 64 & 65. McCoy fan wall pocket. Height 7½" x 8½" wide. Mark: on gold fan, McCoy USA, 24K Gold. Pictured in pink and gold, it was also produced starting in 1957 in lime green, blue, white, and aqua. McCoy produced a line of decorative objects in gold which it named its Starburst Gold line. Estimated value: $25.00 to $40.00 each.

PLATE 66. *McCoy half console bowl wall pocket. Measurements not available. Mark: unknown. Pictured in pink with brown flecks, it also comes in lime green and brown flecks. Not much has been written about this pocket. Estimated value: $20.00 to $30.00.*

PLATE 67 & 68. *McCoy rose wall pocket. Height 6". Unmarked. This wall pocket can also be used as a free standing planter. This pocket came in a variety of color combinations including yellow and pink. The glaze combination used on the right is in what is known as the Rustic glaze. The rose pocket is somewhat more common than other McCoy pockets and easier to find in perfect condition since it does not have applied decorations. This pocket was first produced in 1946. Estimated value: $15.00 to $25.00 each.*

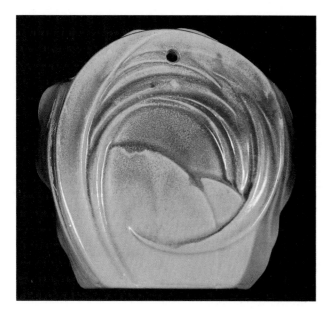

PLATE 69. *This is the back of the McCoy rose wall pocket. As can be seen, the modeled and glazed back suggests that is was also intended to be used as a free standing planter that might be viewed from the back.*

PLATE 70. *McCoy bird on a flower. Height approximately 6". Mark: McCoy. When found, this pocket often has damage as is the case with the one pictured (tail of the bird has been broken off). Estimated value: if perfect $25.00 to $35.00.*

PLATE 71. *McCoy leaf wall pocket. Height 6". Unmarked. This pocket was also produced with an airbrushed blue glaze, in addition to the airbrushed pink shown. Without the hole in the back that makes it a wall pocket, this object was also marketed as a smokeless ashtray. The pictured pocket was picked up at a garage sale for 5 cents! Estimated value: $25.00 to $35.00.*

PLATE 72. McCoy Dutch shoes. Height 7½". Mark: McCoy. This is another fairly common McCoy pocket. These shoes can also be found as planters without a hole for hanging. Estimated value: $15.00 to $20.00.

PLATE 73. McCoy mailbox. Height 7¾". Mark: McCoy, USA. Estimated value: $20.00 to $30.00.

# Hull

The A. E. Hull Pottery was established in Zanesville, Ohio, in 1905. They began producing commercial art pottery around 1920 and started to concentrate on that type of pottery by the mid-1930s.

Hull is noted for its distinctive lines of pastel matte glazes characterized by light blue, pink, and yellow. Hull also used glossy glazes, however.

Hull designed some wall pockets specifically for the kitchen. These include a cup and saucer, iron, whisk-broom, and pitcher. Their commercial art pottery lines generally included wall pockets. For example, wall pockets came in the Camellia, Poppy, Sunglow, Rosella, and Woodland lines. Many pieces are marked Hull USA.

The Hull plant was destroyed in 1950, and a modern plant with new kilns was built. Unfortunately, these new kilns could not duplicate the soft, matte glazes for which Hull was famous. Their newer lines were decorated with shiny glazes. The company went out of business in 1985.

PLATE 74. *Hull Bow-Knot Cup and Saucer. Height 6". Mark:* Hull-Art U.S.A. B-24-6. *Produced in 1949. This lovely matte glaze in pastel colors is very typical of Hull wares. The Bow-Knot line was made in matte glazes that faded from blue to pink or turquoise to blue. Estimated value: $60.00 to $80.00.*

PLATE 75. *Hull Sunglow Pitcher. Height 5½". Mark:* Hull U.S.A. 80. *This line was produced in 1952. Some Sunglow pieces have gold decoration while others do not. The Sunglow line was characterized by shiny glazes. Estimated value: $50.00 to $65.00.*

PLATE 76. *Hull Sunglow Pitcher. Height 5½". Mark:* Hull U.S.A. 81. *The yellow background distinguishes this pocket from PLATE 74. Estimated value: $50.00 to $65.00.*

PLATE 77. Hull Sunglow cup and saucer. Height 6¼".
Mark: Hull U.S.A. 80. Estimated value: $50.00 to
$65.00.

PLATE 78. Hull whisk broom. Height 8".
Mark: impressed U.S.A. 82. This line was produced in the early 1950s. Estimated value:
$45.00 to $60.00.

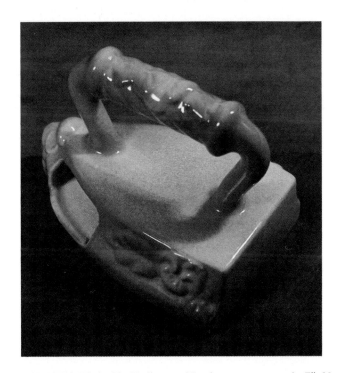

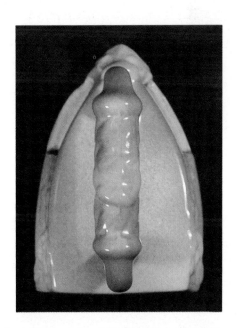

PLATES 79 & 80. Hull iron. Height approximately 7". Unmarked. Estimated value: $45.00 to $60.00.

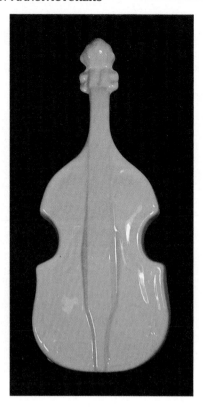

*PLATE 81. Hull violin. Height 7". Mark:* Hull U.S.A. 85. *Estimated value: $40.00 to $50.00.*

*PLATE 82. Hull Hi-Gloss Woodland Shell. Height 7½". Mark:* Hull U.S.A. W13-7½". *This shiny glaze suggests that this was made after the new kilns were installed in the factory and was produced from 1952 to 1954. Dealer price: $125.00.*

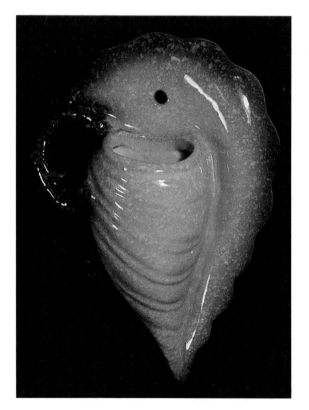

*PLATE 83. Hull Royal Woodland Shell. Height 7½". Mark:* Hull U.S.A. W 13-7½". *This is another piece produced in the 1950s. The Royal line was characterized by a pink or turquoise background with white splattered overglaze decoration. Estimated value: $75.00 to $95.00.*

PLATE 84. *Hull Flying Goose. Height 6" x 7" wide.* Mark: *Hull 67 U.S.A. This shiny glazed pocket in pinks and blues was produced in the early 1950s and was part of Hull's Novelty line. Estimated value: $75.00 to $95.00.*

PLATE 85. *Hull Flying Goose. Height 6" x 7" wide.* Mark: *Hull 67 U.S.A. This pocket is identical to PLATE 84 but in bolder colors of red, black, and green. The Novelty line of which this and PLATE 84 are a part was produced from 1951 to 1960. Estimated value: $75.00 to $95.00.*

PLATE 86. *This is an example of a Hull script mark.*

PLATE 87. *This is a Hull-Art mark. This piece was also identified with a foil paper label that says* Hull Pottery Crooksville, Ohio, *written around the figure of a man at a potter's wheel.*

# Royal Copley

Royal Copley was made by the Spaulding China Company in Sebring, Ohio, from 1942 to 1957. The Royal Copley line was marketed through variety and five-and-ten cent stores. Royal Copley does not have the art pottery look of Weller or Roseville. Many full figures and expressive faces are found in their line of wall pockets. These faces often have a cute or comical look that is particularly appealing. The face pockets sometimes depict persons from other lands. There is a Mexican man in a sombrero, a Chinese girl and boy, a Hindu, a Blackamoor, and a colonial man and woman. Royal Copley pockets always have excellent detail and are carefully painted. Much of the glazing appears airbrushed.

Royal Copley pockets tend to be rather large. They often have a flat bottom that allowed them to be used as regular planters and vases when not hung.

Recently, head vases have become popular collectibles. Because Royal Copley often produced heads that can hang or stand alone, their wall pockets are often offered to the public by dealers as head vases. True head vases were three dimensional and did not hang on the wall. However, because Royal Copley made so many attractive head wall pockets, pocket collectors may find themselves competing with head vase collectors for Royal Copley wares.

Many wall pockets have the mark Royal Copley molded in the back. Others had paper labels.

*PLATES 88 & 89. Oriental boy and girl with hands in sleeves. Height 1½". Unmarked. This delightful pair is typical of the well modeled, expressive features found in Royal Copley wares. Estimated value: $25.00 to $35.00 each.*

*PLATES 90 & 91. Chinese boy and girl. Height 7½". Mark: raised* Royal Copley. *This pair of wall pockets/planters also came in a color combination of gray and red. Estimated value: $25.00 to $35.00 each.*

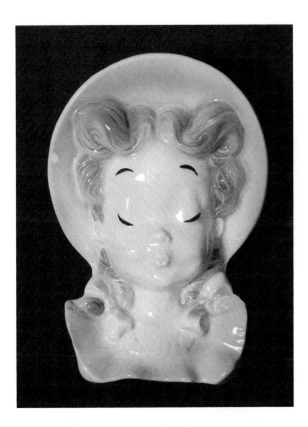

*PLATE 92. Pigtail girl. Height 7". Mark: raised* Royal Copley. *This is a fairly common Royal Copley pocket. It came in several colors — white, blue (shown), and pink. It was also made with a red dress and hat, a color that is more difficult to find. Estimated value: $15.00 to $20.00.*

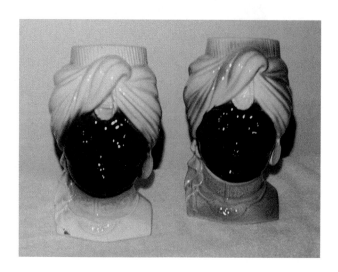

PLATE 93. Blackamoor. Height 8". Mark: raised Royal Copley. Shown with yellow turban. Estimated value: $25.00 to $35.00.

PLATE 94. This picture shows the Blackamoor wall pocket in other color combinations. In addition to the turban fabric cascading over the left shoulder, this handsome pocket came in another, more rare version in which the turban fabric fell over the right shoulder. A different necklace also distinguished the right shoulder version.

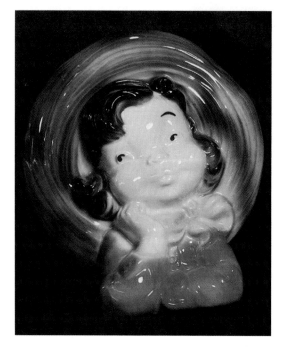

PLATES 95 & 96. Wide brim hat girl and boy. Height 7". Mark: raised Royal Copley. The boy is leaning on his left hand and the girl leans on her right hand. Both have pursed lips. In addition to the color combination of a blue hat and red shirt as shown, these were also made with a chartreuse hat and green shirt. The latter color combination is harder to find. Estimated value: $25.00 to $35.00 each.

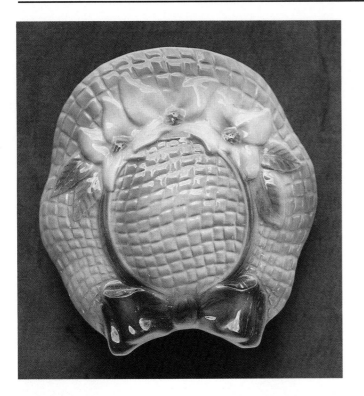

*PLATE 97. Bonnet with flowers. Height 6½". Mark: raised* Royal Copley. *This hat also came in yellow with red flowers. Estimated value: $20.00 to $30.00.*

*PLATE 98. Small bonnet with flowers. Height 5". Mark: raised* Royal Copley. Royal Copley *made this smaller hat adorned with a bow in red, blue, or tan (shown) and decorated with blue, yellow, and red flowers (the red hat had only blue and yellow flowers). Estimated value: $20.00 to $30.00.*

*PLATE 99. Colonial man (sometimes referred to as the old man). Height 8". Mark: raised* Royal Copley. *This is one of a pair that includes a colonial woman wearing a similar hat. She also appears to be old. This man was reproduced in Japan. The Japanese version is unmarked and the glazing is rather garish and inferior to the subtle shading seen in Royal Copley wares. Estimated value $25.00 to $35.00.*

PLATE 100. Cocker spaniel head. Height 8". Paper label. Mark: raised Royal Copley. The company made a variety of wall pockets/planters that featured animals such as dogs, cats, and farm animals. Estimated value $15.00 to $22.00.

PLATE 101. Rooster. Height 6". Mark: raised Royal Copley. Like most of Royal Copley's wall pockets, this one can be used as a free standing planter as well as a wall pocket. This rooster was also produced with brown feathers and a black tail. Estimated value: $25.00 to $35.00.

PLATE 102. Rooster on a plaque. Height 6½". Mark: raised Royal Copley. This pocket has a mate featuring a hen. Another, similarly shaped pocket was also produced with fruit on a plaque. Estimated value: $25.00 to $35.00.

PLATE 103. Apple. Height 6". Mark: raised Royal Copley. This is a well modeled piece with excellent detail. Notice that the leaves are cleverly used to create a foot if it is to be used as a free standing planter rather than a wall pocket. Estimated value: $20.00 to $30.00.

PLATE 104. Pirate. Height 8½". Mark: raised Royal Copley. This handsome figure is a good example of the male heads, often of exotic origins, produced by Royal Copley. In general, males seemed to have been a fairly rare subject for wall pocket manufacturers but Royal Copley produced several men and boys. The pirate is a difficult head pocket to find. In addition to the color combination shown, the pirate was also made with a gray scarf. That color combination is quite rare. Estimated value: $35.00 to $45.00.

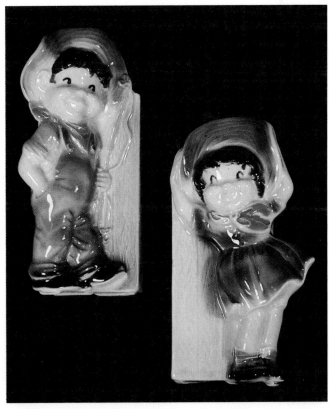

PLATE 105. Boy with a fishing pole and girl with a hat. Height 6". Mark: raised Royal Copley. Mischievous expressions on these children highlight these cute pockets. A collection of Royal Copley's boy and girl pockets would be a clever addition to a child's room. Estimated value: $25.00 to $35.00.

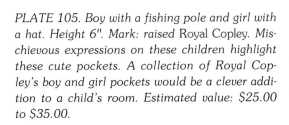

PLATE 106. Angel. Height 6½". Unmarked. This sweet figure is one that would probably look better displayed sitting rather than hung. Nevertheless, it came with a hole for hanging. Estimated value: $20.00 to $30.00.

PLATES 107 & 108. These are examples of Royal Copley raised marks.

# Morton Pottery

Morton, Illinois, was the home of six different potteries whose founders all trace their ancestry to six Rapp brothers who came to the United States from Germany. The first pottery was founded in 1877, and the last pottery ceased operation in 1976. The Morton Pottery Company operated the longest, from 1922 to 1976. Through the 1950s and 1960s, the Morton Pottery Company made many novelty items, among them wall pockets. Most of these pockets are unmarked but most can be identified by a distinctive if not somewhat gaudy glaze combination. The pockets were first dipped in a white glaze and then accents of yellow, blue, red, and turquoise glazes were hand brushed over the white.

Like many other American potteries, the Morton Pottery Company had great difficulty competing with Japanese imports. They finally ceased operation in 1976. A small ceramic gift shop purchased their molds and reproduced some of their lines. It is not known if this shop is still in operation.

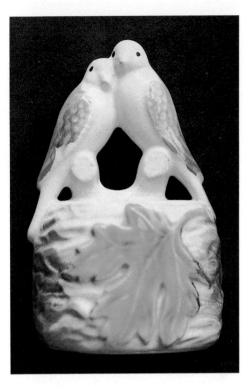

*PLATE 109. Lovebirds on a nest. Height 6½". Unmarked. This is a common Morton Pottery wall pocket and is not difficult to find, particularly in the Midwest. This pocket has a flat bottom so that it can be utilized as a free standing planter. Estimated value: $15.00 to $20.00.*

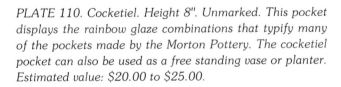

*PLATE 110. Cocketiel. Height 8". Unmarked. This pocket displays the rainbow glaze combinations that typify many of the pockets made by the Morton Pottery. The cocketiel pocket can also be used as a free standing vase or planter. Estimated value: $20.00 to $25.00.*

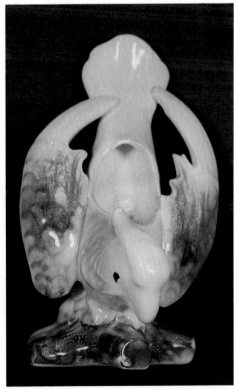

PLATE 112. Owl on the moon. Height 7½". Unmarked. This rather hard-to-find pocket can be hung or can stand alone. The backside also has modeling so that it can be viewed from either side. Both tips of the moon are broken off on the pocket pictured. Estimated value: in perfect condition $20.00 to $30.00.

PLATE 111. Parrot with grapes. Height 8½". Unmarked. This colorful pocket can be somewhat difficult to find. Estimated value: $20.00 to $30.00.

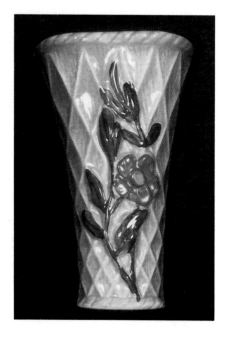

PLATES 113 & 114. Flower on a basket. Height 7½". Unmarked. These are very common wall pockets by this company and were made in a variety of glaze colors. Estimated value: $15.00 to $20.00.

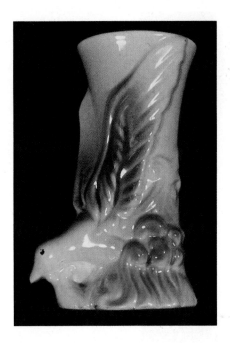

PLATE 115. Bird. Height 7½". Unmarked. Estimated
value: $15.00 to $20.00.

PLATES 116 & 117. Rooster and hen. Height 8". Unmarked. This pair was made in other glaze combinations including the flowing glazes used in PLATE 115. Estimated value: $25.00 to $35.00 each.

PLATE 118. Bird with house. Height 5¾". Unmarked. This little pocket, like many made by this company, will stand alone if not hung. It was made with several glaze colors accenting the roof and the bird. Estimated value: $10.00 to $15.00.

PLATE 119. Peacocks. Height 6½". Mark: U.S.A. These peacocks were also produced in pink and white. Estimated value: $10.00 to $15.00.

# Shawnee Pottery Company

The Shawnee Pottery Company, maker of cookie jars and the popular King Corn line, also produced an assortment of wall pockets. The company, which operated in Zanesville, Ohio, from 1937 to 1961, produced inexpensive novelty items, many of which have airbrushed decoration. The wall pockets often have flat bottoms that allow them to be used as free standing planters as well as wall hung vases. It is not unusual for Shawnee wall pockets to be unmarked which may make them difficult to identify.

*PLATE 120. Birdhouse with birds. Height approximately 5". Mark: Shawnee 800 Series, 830. Most Shawnee pockets have airbrushed decoration. Notice how the colors were also sprayed onto the background indicating that these were quickly and inexpensively produced. This pocket was also made with red birds and a blue house. Estimated value: $20.00 to $30.00.*

*PLATE 121. Little Jack Horner. Height 5". Mark: USA 585. Many Shawnee pockets have USA as part of the mark. This pocket is one of a pair. The mate is Little Bo Peep. Estimated value: $15.00 to $20.00.*

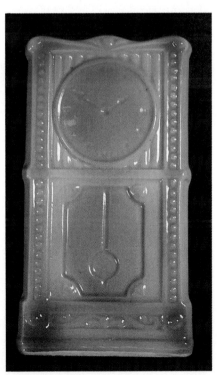

*PLATE 122. Grandfather clock. Height 6½". Mark: USA 126. Like make Shawnee wall pockets this one can also stand alone as a planter. Estimated value: $30.00 to $40.00.*

PLATE 123. Scotty dog. Height 9" x 5" wide. Unmarked. This pocket was one of the first pieces designed by Louise Bauer in 1937, for Shawnee. It was produced in white, blue, green, burgundy, and yellow. The pocket pictured is actually white but it has been cold painted in gold with black eyes. It is not known if this is a factory finish or was done by an owner with artistic delusions. Estimated value: if perfect $30.00 to $35.00.

PLATE 124. Red feather wall pocket. Height 5". Unmarked. This is apparently a rather rare Shawnee pocket. Estimated value: $40.00 to $50.00 according to Jim and Beverly Mangus in their book, Shawnee Pottery: Identification and Price Guide. 1994. This pocket was bought for $5.00, however.

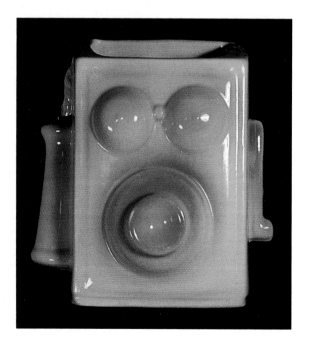

PLATE 125. Wallphone. Height 6". Mark: U.S.A. 529. Estimated value: $30.00 to $35.00.

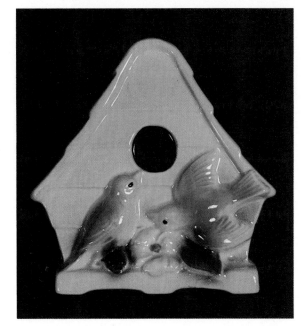

PLATE 126. Birds and house. Height 5½". Mark: 39 circled. This mark is different from other Shawnee marks but is believed to have been produced by the company. This was also produced with blue birds. Estimated value: $15.00 to $25.00.

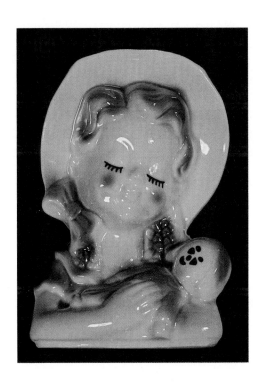

PLATE 127. Girl with rag doll. Height 6½". Mark: U.S.A. 810. Estimated value: $15.00 to $25.00.

# Other American Potteries

Over the last hundred years, many American potteries have produced wall pockets as a part of their decorative lines. While they may not have produced pockets in large enough numbers to merit a collection of their own, they are often represented in larger, mixed collections.

The Abingdon Pottery Company, producer of sanitary ware, added an art ware division in 1934. From that time to 1950, they produced several lines of art pottery, cookie jars, and novelties. They used several marks that generally included the company name.

George Brush went into business with J. W. McCoy in 1909, to form the Brush-McCoy Pottery Company in Zanesville, Ohio. This pottery produced commercial wares as well as several lines of fine art pottery. Wall pockets were produced by the Brush-McCoy Pottery Company. After McCoy died, his family withdrew from the business, and in 1925, the company became known as the Brush Pottery Company. By that time few companies still produced hand-decorated art ware and the Brush Company became most famous for its cookie jars. However, the Brush Company also produced wall pockets. These are often found with a Brush molded script mark.

Many small potteries sprang up in and around Los Angeles, California, around 1930. Like the Midwest, this area of California offered the right combination of raw materials for pottery and glazes and cheap fuel for firing to make a ceramics industry a success. Aided by the growing film industry, the economy in that area offered a rare opportunity for growth to these potteries during the depression. During World War II, the lack of foreign competition kept these industries thriving. By 1948, when the pottery industry was at its height in California, there were over 800 potteries in business in the Los Angeles area. This was more than was even found in Ohio, a state often thought of as the heart of the pottery industry in America. Many of the wall pockets made by the various California potteries have a folksy, hand-decorated look. The name of the state is often a part of the mark.

The Camden Art and Tie Company — commonly known as Camark — of Camden, Arkansas, came into being in 1926. They lured one of Weller's designers to Arkansas and began producing art pottery much like that of Weller and J.B. Owens. Within a few years, the focus of the company switched to commercial wares using glossy or matte glazes. These wares were mold cast and made in volume. The early art pottery is very rare and collectible. Collectors are also very interested in their later commercial wares. Camark made a line of animals that is particularly sought after. This line included a large number of cats. Camark's climbing cats decorated trees and the sides of houses. The original pottery closed in 1960.

Oklahoma was the home of the Frank Pottery which became Frankoma in 1934. Frankoma wares can usually be identified by their distinctive, southwestern themes. Until 1954, the pottery used a buff colored clay known as Ada clay. After that time, a red brick clay was used. The earlier, Ada clay is generally more collectible. The color of the clay body and the color of the glazes can be used to date Frankoma items. Frankoma made a variety of wall pockets, most of which have a western or cowboy theme. They make a nice collection for a boy's room or with the currently popular western, Roy Rogers decorating look. Frankoma pockets are generally marked. Frankoma was family run until 1991. The pottery is still in business. This pottery is fairly common in the Southwest but may be more difficult to find on the coasts.

The Redwing Potteries took its name from Red Wing, Minnesota, where it was located. The pottery was founded in 1878. They offered an art ware line in the 1930s and later produced cookie jars and dinnerware. Most wall pockets seem to date from that later period. The Red Wing Pottery closed in 1967.

Little has been published about the Burley Winter pottery company. The appearance of their wares suggests that they produced pottery during the same time frame as the other, better known art potteries of the first half of the century. When identified, their wares have a mottled, two-toned, matte glaze that is rather similar to the glazes in the early Carnelian II line by Roseville. Burley Winter wares apparently were frequently unmarked.

*PLATE 128. Abingdon acanthus leaf. Height 8¾" x 8" wide. This is one of several wall pockets by this company listed in Schroeder's Antiques Price Guide. Estimated value: $25.00 to $35.00.*

*PLATE 129. Brush duck. Height unknown. This pocket was first introduced in 1939. Estimated value: $45.00 to $75.00.*

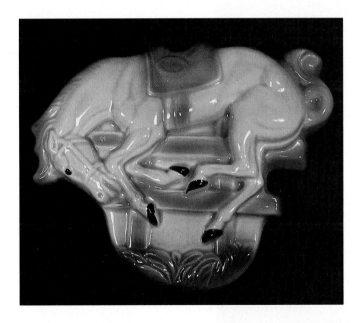

*PLATE 130. Brush bucking horse. Height 7". Mark: 801 USA. Estimated value: $75.00 to $120.00.*

PLATE 131. *Brush wise owl. Height unknown. Mark: unknown. This pocket is decorated with airbrushed, matte glaze. It has a rather textured, almost rough feel to the body. It was manufactured in 1929. Estimated value: $125.00 to $175.00.*

PLATE 132. *Brush cornucopia. Height 7½". Unmarked. This pocket is seen from time to time in other glaze colors besides yellow. Estimated value: $25.00 to $35.00.*

PLATE 133. *Green skillet. Height approximately 7". Mark: Jan's California. California potteries seemed to be fond of applied decorations. Estimated value: $15.00 to $25.00.*

PLATE 134. Black pocket on plate with rose cane decoration. Height approximately 7". Mark: Wm. Frazier #138, 1952, California. Estimated value: $20.00 to $35.00.

PLATE 135. Mallard duck wall pocket or planter. Height 6" x 7" wide. Mark: California Pottery. Estimated value: $20.00 to $35.00.

PLATE 136. Elf by a well. Height 5". Mark: paper label Treasure Craft Original, South Gate California. Estimated value: $20.00 to $30.00.

PLATE 137. Elf on a leaf. Height 7½". Unmarked. This was also made by Treasure Craft in California. Note the similarities in the elves' hats and belt buckles in this and PLATE 136. The green glazes are also the same. Estimated value: $20.00 to $30.00.

PLATE 138. Elf on green grapes. Height 7¾". Mark: Gilner, California. Notice the difference in the hats on the Treasure Craft elves and the hats on the Gilner elves. Estimated value: $25.00 to $35.00.

PLATE 139. Elf on bananas. Height 7½". Mark: Gilner, California. Estimated value: $25.00 to $35.00.

PLATE 140. Elf with chef's hat on grapes. Height 5½". Mark: Gilner, California. Gilner's elves all have little bows at their necks. The chef's hat makes this little guy somewhat unique. Estimated value: $25.00 to $35.00.

PLATE 141. *Troll in a stump. Height 8".*
*Mark: California Pottery Co. Estimated*
*value: $25.00 to $35.00.*

PLATE 142. *Green cuckoo clock. Height 8"*
*without the clock weights. Mark:* Made In
California. *This is somewhat reminiscent of the*
*cuckoo clock produced by McCoy. This version*
*has nice, sharp detail. Estimated value: $20.00*
*to $30.00.*

PLATE 143. *Cross-eyed bear. Height 6". Mark:*
Doranne Calif. BE 14. *The details on this pocket*
*were highlighted by first painting a brown under-*
*glaze on the bisque piece then partially wiping it*
*away leaving the brown in the crevices. The piece*
*was then covered with a clear glaze and fired. Esti-*
*mated value: $25.00 to $35.00.*

*PLATE 144. Fruit pockets on leaves. Height 5".
Mark: Made In California written in script. One
could have a large collection by concentrating
only on fruit pockets on leaves made by the various manufacturers around the country. Estimated
value: $15.00 to $20.00 each.*

*PLATE 145. Indonesian Buddha mask and Balinese
Dancer mask. Height 7½" for woman, 7" for man.
Mark: California Arts, Balinese Dancer Mask on
woman, California Arts, Indonesian Buddha Mask on
man. These beautifully modeled pockets have a very
50s California look. Estimated value: $35.00 to
$45.00 for the pair.*

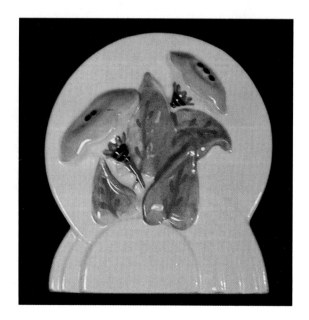

*PLATE 146. Morning Glories. Height 5¾". Mark:
Block Pottery #2, California. Estimated value: $15.00
to $20.00.*

PLATE 147. Scoop wall pocket. Height 8". Mark: Camark, USA. This pocket was also produced in a pink glaze and possibly other colors as well. Estimated value: $10.00 to $15.00.

PLATE 148. Cat. Height approximately 10". Mark: Camark. This unusual cat pocket appears to be climbing up the wall. The pocket opening is in the cat's chest, obscured by the cat's head in this picture. Camark made a number of climbing cats not all of which were wall pockets. Estimated value: $30.00 to $45.00.

PLATE 149. Cup and saucer. Height 7½". Mark: paper label in the shape of Arkansas, Camark Pottery. The origin of these large cup and saucer pockets had always been a mystery to me until I ran across this one with the label intact in Dan Leslie's collection. These are a relatively common pocket, at least in the South and Southwest. Estimated value: $15.00 to $25.00.

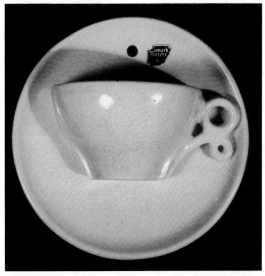

PLATE 150. Camark cup and saucer. Height 7½". Unmarked. This two-toned combination is harder to find than the single color pockets. Estimated value: $20.00 to $30.00.

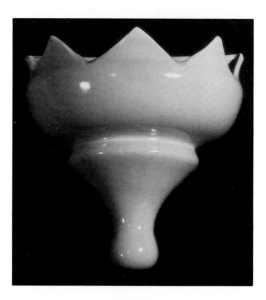

PLATE 151. Large pink wall pocket. Height 7¾". Mark: Molded Camark N35. Estimated value: $20.00 to $30.00.

PLATE 152. Frankoma acorn wall pocket. Height 6". Mark: unknown. This acorn pocket was also made in a smaller version. This is a very typical looking Frankoma glaze. Estimated value: $12.00 to $15.00.

PLATES 153, 154 & 155. Redwing violin. Height 13½". Mark: Redwing USA, M1484. This pocket has a very 50s look to it that is quite charming. In addition to the three colors shown, it was also produced in a pink speckled glaze. The violins that still have their original strings will probably be more valuable than those without. Notice that the pocket on the right still has its original paper label on the front. Estimated value: $15.00 to $25.00.

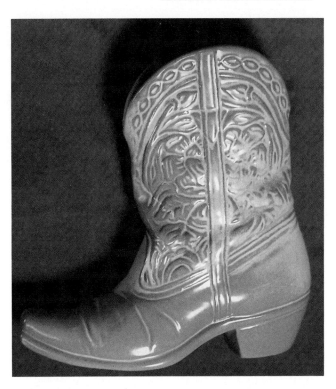

*PLATES 156 & 157. Frankoma boot. Height 6½". Mark: unknown. These boots are made to face each other and are glazed in typical Frankoma colors. The boot wall pocket came in a smaller size and came in various colors, including pink (perhaps for the little girl buckaroo!). These boots are glazed and have the design on the back as well as the front. It is sometimes seen as a free standing bank and the same mold could have been used for both. Estimated value: $12.00 to $15.00 each.*

*PLATE 158. Burley Winters wall hanging crocus pot. Height 3½" x 6" wide. Unmarked. This pocket was made by a rather obscure art pottery maker about whom little has been written. Estimated value: $75.00 to $100.00.*

# European Manufacturers

Many countries of Europe have strong ceramic traditions. The wall pocket collector may find pockets from these European countries from time to time.

## Czechoslovakia

The country of Czechoslovakia was created in 1918, and therefore, wall pockets marked as Czechoslovakian were produced after that date. Czechoslovakia was famous for its glass production and glass wall pockets were also created. Lovely ceramic wall pockets were also produced in that country. Some of these pockets are luster and are similar in appearance to Japanese luster pockets. Another frequently seen type of pocket features birds perched by a nest or birdhouse. These pockets were decorated with a matte glaze that has an airbrushed appearance. Still other pockets have a distinctive folk art look.

With the collapse of the Soviet empire, Czechoslovakia again became a free country. In 1993 it ceased to exist as a unified country when it was divided into the Czechoslovakian Republic and the Slovak Republic. Undoubtedly, wall pockets with the mark of a country that existed for only 75 years will become more valuable.

*PLATE 160. Czech folk art wall pocket. Height 8".* Mark: J. Mrazek, Peasant Art Industry, Made In Czechoslovakia, 135.K. *This large, beautiful pocket is hand decorated in a colorful folk art style. This pocket was pictured in an old advertisement for this company. The background in that picture was green rather than orange. Czech pottery decorated in this style is highly sought after by collectors. Estimated value: $50.00 to $65.00.*

*PLATE 159. Orange wall pocket. Height 5⅜". Mark:* Trademark Coronet, Czechoslovakia Registered. *This pocket is trimmed in black. Orange seemed to be a popular color in Czech pottery. Estimated value: $20.00 to $30.00.*

PLATE 161. Czech luster bird. Height 6". Mark: ink stamp Made In Czechoslovakia, impressed numbers 6080, also ink stamped numbers 31. Luster pockets such as these are very similar to the luster bird pockets produced in Japan. The colors on this pocket are airbrushed and the luster is in excellent condition. Estimated value: $35.00 to $50.00.

PLATE 162. Czech bird by a birdhouse. Height 6". Mark: ink stamp Made In Czechoslovakia. This pocket is very typical of the many small bird pockets produced in Czechoslovakia. The glazes are airbrushed and have a satin rather than shiny finish to them. Estimated value: $35.00 to $50.00.

PLATE 163. Czech bird on a limb. Height 6". Mark: ink stamp Made In Czechoslovakia. The tip of the bird's tail is chipped on this pocket, a flaw that should be watched for in any bird pocket. Note that this pocket has three openings. Estimated value: if perfect $35.00 to $50.00.

*PLATE 164. Czech bird by a nest. Height 6". Mark: ink stamp* Made In Czechoslovakia. *This is another typical style Czech bird pocket with airbrushed decoration and two openings. Estimated value: $35.00 to $50.00.*

*PLATE 165. Owl on a castle. Height 5½". Mark: ink stamp* Made In Czechoslovakia *also impressed 6082. This little pocket is less frequently seen than the other bird pockets shown here. Estimated value: $35.00 to $50.00.*

*PLATE 166. Bird with long tail. Height 7". Mark: ink stamp* Made In Czechoslovakia, *ink stamp 32, impressed 5952A. Estimated value: $35.00 to $50.00.*

# Germany

Wall pockets in porcelain and bisque were produced by various manufacturers in Germany. Many porcelain pockets were simply marked "Germany." Between the two world wars, luster wall pockets made of porcelain were produced in Germany that look very much like Japanese luster pockets. There are some subtle differences in glaze and luster colors but the collector must primarily depend on a discernible mark to distinguish between the two.

Bisque is a type of unglazed earthenware or porcelain that has only been fired once. Bisque wall pockets were decorated in pastel colors and accented in gold. These pockets were often unmarked.

One of the great ceramic manufacturers of Germany that produces wall pockets is the Goebel company. Three pockets were produced in their famous Hummel line. These are considered quite rare by Hummel collectors although they are now back in production. The three wall pockets, one of a boy, one of a girl, and one of a boy and a girl, were originally designed by Goebel's master sculptor Gerhart Skrobek in 1959. Collectors of Hummels can discriminate the age of their collectibles by the mark used.

*PLATE 167. German bisque green and white pocket. Height approximately 7". Mark: Germany. This pocket shows a very strong influence of Wedgwood Jasperware. Jasperware is a bisque fired stoneware decorated with white classical figures in low relief. This pocket can also be found in Wedgwood blue and white. Estimated value: $65.00 to $75.00.*

*PLATE 168 (left). German bisque angel. Height 7¼". Unmarked. This expressive little cherub with her purple brushed bow and demur drape looks very Victorian. She is very similar in style and decoration to bisque figurines made during that era to adorn mantles. Estimated value: $60.00 to $75.00.*

*PLATE 169 (right). Goebel umbrella pocket. Height 7". Mark: Goebel with crown and full bee mark. The mark dates this pocket to the 1930s. It is one of a pair and was made by the company that produces Hummels. Estimated value: $45.00 to $55.00.*

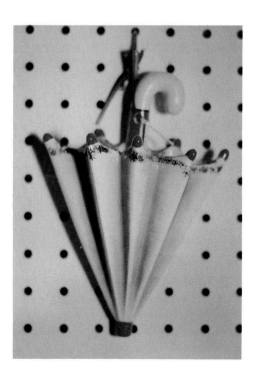

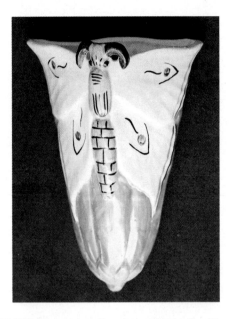

PLATE 170. German yellow luster butterfly. Height 5¾".
Mark: impressed Germany. This butterfly perched on a
flower could easily be mistaken for a Japanese pocket if
it were not marked otherwise. Estimated value: $25.00
to $35.00.

PLATE 172. 17th century woman. Height 7". Mark: Germany. Sometimes you have to look hard for the Germany
mark. The impressed mark is often filled with glaze and
somewhat obscured. They generally seem to be found at
the bottom of the back side of the pocket. Estimated
value: $30.00 to $40.00.

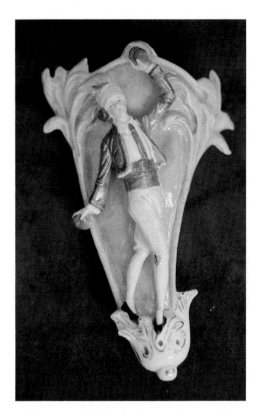

PLATE 171. Spanish dancer. Height 7½". Mark:
impressed Germany. This intricate pocket with its deli-
cate male dancer and exotic background seems a rather
odd design choice for a German manufacturer but it
reflects the interest in art deco of the 1920s and 1930s.
Estimated value: $30.00 to $40.00.

# England

England has a long and well-documented ceramic arts tradition. England was instrumental in the industrial evolution of the ceramic arts, and its pottery industry had a world-wide impact on Western ceramic production. Many potteries were located in the Staffordshire region. Wedgwood was particularly important in contributing to the ceramic industry. Many of the lovely majolica wallpockets pictured in this book were produced in England in the 1800s. As in the United States, potteries in England sprang up in areas where clay was plentiful and fuel was available for kilns.

Many of the wall pockets available to the collector (aside from the early majolica pockets) were produced from about the turn of the century through the early 1950s with breaks for the wars. Potteries in England are still in production and produce new pockets from time to time. Older wall pockets may be marked with the English diamond shaped registry mark. Later works will be marked "England" or "Made in England."

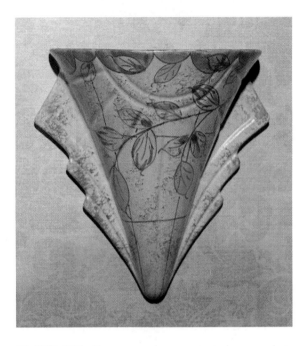

PLATE 173. *Orange and cream art deco pocket. Height 6½" x 6¼" wide. Mark:* Fenton, Kensington-ware, Made In England. *This pocket has the geometric lines common in art deco design. Estimated value: $30.00 to $40.00.*

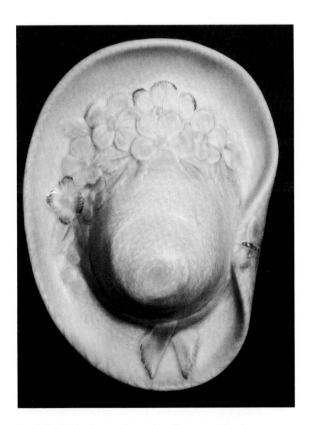

PLATE 174. *Green hat with flowers. Height approximately 6". Mark:* Made In England Beswick, 651. *A lovely pocket in pastel colors, this pocket is suggestive of the English countryside. Dealer price: $85.00.*

# Holland

Most pottery from this country is produced near the town of Gouda. Gouda art pottery has a distinctive, Art Nouveau look and was first produced around 1885. Geometric shapes as well as stylized birds and florals can be found in Gouda wares. This pottery is generally glazed in a matte finish but gloss glazes were also used and are the highest priced. Pottery made in Gouda is still being produced although the majority of the original potteries failed during the depression of the 1930s. Most of this pottery, regardless of the particular pottery producing it, has the name Gouda in the mark.

PLATE 176. Gouda art deco pocket. Height approximately 7". Mark: stamped Gouda, also Olra Arnhem-Holland-477. This pocket exhibits the bright colored, matte glazes often seen in Gouda pottery from Holland. Antique show price: $295.00.

PLATE 175. Conical Gouda pocket. Height 8¾". Mark: Gouda. Gouda pottery from Holland was often decorated in an art deco manner such as this. Estimated value: $125.00.

## France

There have been several pottery centers in France. These were located where there was sufficient clay, water, and wood to support a pottery industry. Unlike England, there is no national pottery mark for France. The word "Deposee," which means registered, is sometimes found on French wares along with a manufacturer's mark.

Majolica wall pockets from France are sometimes found as well as those produced in other styles such as Quimper.

PLATE 177. Quimper rolled cone pocket. Height unknown. Mark: Quimper. The decoration on this pocket is a good example of the style of this French made pottery. Estimated value: $165.00.

# Portugal

Portugal has a long history of ceramic production. A center for ceramic manufacture is Caldas de Rainha (the queen's bath), a town north of Lisbon. Majolica wall pockets produced during the late 1800s can be seen in the section on majolica in this book. These often have a rough, textured look with undulating reptiles, exotic animals, plants, and flowers. Reproductions of the majolica made in Portugal during the Victorian era are again being made and are generally marked PORTUGAL. Some new wall pockets are also being made although those seen by the author have a vegetable motif.

# Italy

Italy still exports considerable pottery and porcelain. Wall pockets can be found in the brightly colored folk art style often seen in Italian tiles. Another popular export is Capo-Di-Monte. This ware was first produced by a factory in Naples in the 1700s and the original factory closed in 1821. A factory in Florence purchased some of the original molds and continues to produce these wares. Most Capo-Di-Monte imported into the United States is new and of inferior quality to the original.

PLATE 178. Portuguese turnips. Height 12". Mark: paper label Bordalo Piheiro, Caldas Da Rainha, Made In Portugal. These large, kitchen-themed wall pockets can be found in other designs as well. They were recently offered in an exclusive gift catalog. Estimated value: $20.00 to $35.00.

PLATE 179. Italian Capo-Di-Monte. Height 14½". Mark: crown over an N, also Capodimonte, Made in Italy. The mark of a crown over an "N" has become the traditional mark for Capo-Di-Monte style wares, some of which are not made in Italy. This wall pocket appears to be fairly new. Estimated value: $15.00 to $25.00.

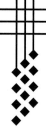

# Mexico

Much of Mexico's ceramics have a folk art look that reflects the country's historic ties to Spain. Wall pockets can be found in a variety of styles that have been imported from Mexico, especially in the Southwest. Large wall hung, terra cotta planters that are produced in Mexico can be purchased in garden centers. Smaller wall pockets can be found that are glazed and hand decorated. The wall pockets pictured may have been originally produced with the domestic Mexican market in mind.

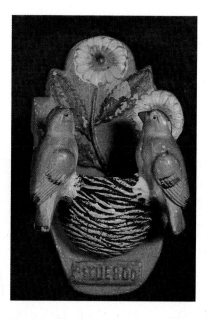

*PLATE 180. Blue birds on pink background. Height 5¾". Unmarked. This pocket is very similar to PLATE 181. Both are rather crudely made and decorated. This pocket also has RECUERDO printed on the front which indicates that it was produced as a souvenir. Estimated value: $10.00 to $15.00.*

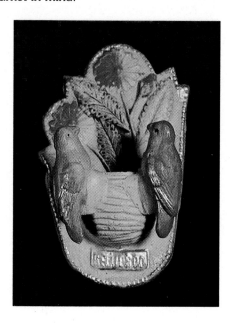

*PLATE 181. Yellow nest with pink birds. Height 5¾". Mark: Made In Mexico. This is cold paint decoration over a low fired bisque body. The word on the front is RECUERDO which means souvenir in Spanish. Estimated value: $10.00 to $15.00.*

*PLATE 182. Green birds on a nest. Height 7". Unmarked. This style of pocket can be found, especially in the Southwest, from time to time. Because they are generally unmarked, collectors and dealers are often confused by their origin. I have seen them identified as the work of Weller although these look nothing like the beautifully crafted pockets by that American company. Although generally moderately priced, I have also seen them priced as high as $95.00. Estimated value: $20.00 to $35.00.*

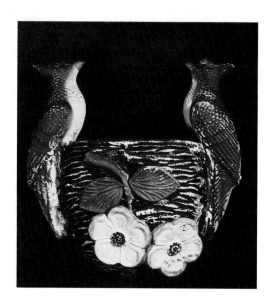

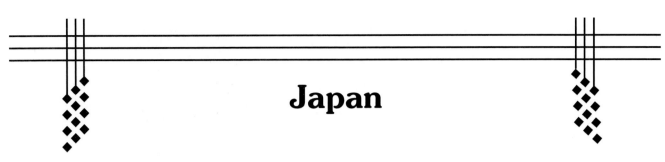

# Japan

By far the most prolific producer of wall pockets over the years has been Japan. Starting after World War I, Japan exported hundreds of different styles of wall pockets to the United States. Especially during the 1920s, vases, sugar castors, lamps, and tea sets were imported into this country and often given away as subscription premiums to individuals who sold magazines. These wares were also sold in gift shops, by mail order, and in 5 and 10 cent stores.

Because these wares were inexpensive and readily available, many people came to see Japanese wares as cheap and of poor quality. Actually, most wares were hand decorated by small, family-owned businesses and show considerable finesse and attention to detail.

The majority of these pockets will have a mark that says "Made in Japan" or simply, "Japan." From 1891 to 1921, wares from Japan were marked "Nippon." In 1921 the United States government required that imports be marked "Japan." This quirk of the import law allows us to date most Japanese pockets as being produced after 1921. During World War II (at least after the bombing of Pearl Harbor), imports from Japan to the U.S. ceased. After the war, beginning in 1947, Japanese wares had to be identified as "Made in Occupied Japan." This identification was used until 1952. All porcelain marked "Made in Occupied Japan" has become very collectible. Wall pockets are no exception.

Collectors sometimes wonder why two wall pockets may be identical in size and shape and yet have different glazes and marks. "Made in Japan" may be in a different ink color or there is a totally different, decorative mark. One explanation is that one company often cast the pocket. This company would often impress "Made in Japan" into the back of the wall pocket while the clay was still wet. Other small companies would then buy the blanks (as the undecorated, bisque wall pockets were called) and decorate them with their own glaze colors and lusters. These companies would often add their own ink backstamp.

The Noritake Company produced beautifully lustered porcelain during the era between the world wars. In a Noritake catalog, the company advertised a variety of wall pockets. One Noritake ad for wall pockets read "A decidedly smart means of displaying decorative flowers." Collecting Noritake porcelain is an obsession all to itself. Collecting Noritake wall pockets is still "decidedly smart."

The most common colors were mother of pearl luster (white overlaid with luster), blue, and amber, These luster colors are seen again and again in Japanese wall pockets with a porcelain body. These represent the largest single group of wall pockets on the market today. Yellow luster and an intense reddish-orange are also common colors on these pockets. Japanese luster ware pockets with more unusual colors will probably become more collectible. Some wonderful Oriental designs are decorated with moriage ( a raised slip decoration) and gold.

In addition to characteristic glaze color, Japanese luster ware pockets tended to have similar design motifs. One of the most common was birds. All kinds of birds can be found in luster ware — bluebirds, geese, cranes, owls, peacocks, woodpeckers, cuckoos, birds of paradise, and all types of parrots and parakeets. Japanese luster ware bird pockets are collected exclusively by some individuals.

Other wonderful and fanciful designs are also found in luster ware. Boats or butterflies may sail across a wall. A fly or ladybug may cling to a wall. An elephant may stand ready to step into the room. Children are frequently depicted in these wall pockets. These were obviously designed for the American or European market with Caucasian rather than Oriental features.

Not all pockets imported from Japan were lustered. Many examples of porcelain and pottery pockets are merely glazed. These glazed pockets show more diversity of color. They are often in somewhat pastel shades popular in the art deco era of the thirties. People are often depicted in these unlustered versions. Other pockets in this category sometimes have runny glazes somewhat like majolica. These are even represented by the unscrupulous or unknowing dealer as "Japanese majolica." Never pay majolica prices for

Japanese wall pockets. They are definitely wonderful but they are not particularly rare and they are not majolica.

Another rather common Japanese wall pocket was made with a gray clay body. These pockets typically have bright, shiny glazes in shades of blue, green, yellow, red, and mauve. These pockets are generally quite lightweight and are sometimes referred to as "Banko Ware." While they do not appear to be the traditional Banko Ware produced in Japan, dealers and collectors sometimes describe them as such. Birds and flowers are common design motifs for these wall pockets. A fairly common pair of pockets of this type depict a Japanese man and woman dressed in traditional Japanese costumes and carrying baskets on their backs. The price of these particular pockets has risen dramatically in the last two years.

Another class of Japanese wall pocket was also made with a gray clay body that is thicker than the previously described type. These pockets are often black with molded decorations. The design motifs often appear to be in traditional Japanese style or less often, art deco. While most have a black background, other colors are sometimes seen as well. They all appear to be cold painted rather than glazed and often have painted gold highlights. This style was made to imitate a type of cloisonné known as "tree bark cloisonné."

The Japanese produced many wall pockets featuring birds. These are as a group, the most common pockets a collector can find. Birds make a wonderful collection of their own.

*PLATE 183. Bird wall pocket. Height 6¾". Mark: impressed in circle* Made in Japan. *Estimated value: $20.00 to $25.00.*

*PLATE 185. Bird wall pocket. Height 6¼". Mark: ink stamped* Made in Japan. *Estimated value: $20.00 to $25.00.*

*PLATE 184. Bird wall pocket. Height 6". Mark: impressed* Made in Japan. *Estimated value: $15.00 to $20.00.*

*PLATE 186. Bird wall pocket. Height 6¾". Mark: impressed* Made in Japan. *Estimated value: $20.00 to $25.00.*

*PLATE 187. Parrot. Height 7¾". Mark: impressed* Made in Japan. *Estimated value: $25.00 to $35.00.*

*PLATE 188. Parrot. Height 9½". Mark: impressed* Made in Japan. *Estimated value: $25.00 to $35.00.*

*PLATE 189. Long-billed bird. Height 8". Mark:* Made in Japan. *Estimated value: $25.00 to $35.00.*

PLATE 190. Long-billed bird. Height 9¾". Mark: impressed Made in Japan. Estimated value: $25.00 to $35.00.

PLATE 191. Bird wall pocket. Height 9". Mark: ink stamp Made in Japan. This pocket has beautiful glaze colors that are reminiscent of English majolica. Estimated value: $30.00 to $40.00.

PLATE 192. Bird wall pocket. Height 8". Mark: ink stamp Made in Japan. This pocket appears to be identical in shape to PLATE 191 but is an inch shorter. Estimated value: $30.00 to $40.00.

*PLATE 193. Owl. Height 7". Mark: impressed* Made in Japan. *Estimated value: $25.00 to $30.00.*

*PLATE 194. Parrot. Height 9¾". Mark: circular impressed* Made in Japan. *Estimated value: $25.00 to $35.00.*

*PLATE 195. Peacock. Height 10". Mark: impressed* Made in Japan. *Estimated value: $30.00 to $40.00.*

PLATE 196. Bird wall pocket. Height 10". Mark: impressed Made in Japan. Estimated value: $30.00 to $40.00.

PLATE 197. Mother bird with chicks. Height 7½". Mark: impressed Made in Japan. Estimated value: $25.00 to $30.00.

PLATE 198. Mother bird with chicks. Height 9½". Mark: impressed Made in Japan. PLATES 197 and 198 appear very much alike but the pocket in PLATE 198 is 1½" longer. There are subtle differences in the design with the pocket in PLATE 197 having sharper and better detail. Estimated value: $25.00 to $35.00.

PLATE 199. *Bird wall pocket. Height 6¾". Mark: ink stamp* Made in Japan. *Estimated value: $20.00 to $25.00.*

PLATE 200. *Bird wall pocket. Height 6¾". Mark: impressed* Made in Japan. *Estimated value: $20.00 to $25.00.*

PLATE 201. *Bird on yellow branch. Height 7". Mark: impressed* Made in Japan. *Estimated value: $20.00 to $25.00.*

PLATE 202. *Cockatoo. Height unknown. Mark: impressed* Made in Japan. *This pocket has interesting, very three dimensional modeling that makes it rather unique. Estimated value: $30.00 to $40.00.*

PLATE 203. Turquoise bird. Height 5¼". Mark: ink stamp Made in Japan. Estimated value: $20.00 to $25.00.

PLATE 204. Parrot on a perch. Height 9". Mark: circular impressed Made in Japan. This rather contemplative fellow was apparently decorated quickly. Note the red glaze splashed on his breast. Estimated value: $30.00 to $40.00.

PLATE 205. Bird with flowers. Height 8½". Mark: ink stamp Made in Japan. Estimated value: $25.00 to $35.00.

PLATE 206. Bird wall pocket. Height 5". Mark: ink stamp Made in Japan. Estimated value: $20.00 to $25.00.

PLATE 207. Bird with grapes. Height 5½". Mark: ink stamp Made in Japan. The beautiful glazes on this pocket make it very eye catching. Estimated value: $25.00 to $35.00.

PLATE 208. Bird with grapes. Height 5". Mark: green ink stamp with flower logo, Hand Paint, Made in Japan. It must have been common for one manufacturer to rip off the designs of another company. PLATES 207 and 208 are so similar but are different heights and have different marks. Note the fine, hand-applied detail on this bird's head and wings. Estimated value: $25.00 to $35.00.

PLATE 209. Parrot on a perch. Height 8½". Unmarked. Estimated value: $25.00 to $35.00.

PLATE 210. Parrot on a perch. Height 8". Mark: impressed Made in Japan. Again, PLATES 209 and 210 appear very similar but are different heights and have different types of glazes. The glazes on this pocket are more transparent and the underlying body color appears speckled. Estimated value: $25.00 to $35.00.

PLATE 211. Parrot on a perch. Height 9¾". Mark: impressed Made in Japan. Estimated value: $30.00 to $35.00.

PLATE 212. Cockatoo on a perch. Height 9½". Mark: circular impressed Made in Japan. Estimated value: $30.00 to $35.00.

PLATE 213. Parrot on a perch. Height 9½". Unmarked. It is very unusual for Japanese pockets to be unmarked. This may have had a paper label that has disappeared. Estimated value: $25.00 to $35.00.

PLATE 214. *Bird on grapes. Height 6½". Mark: ink stamp* Made in Japan. *Estimated value: $15.00 to $20.00.*

PLATE 215. *Bird on leaves. Height 7". Unmarked. I'm assuming that this is Japanese but it also looks a bit different from other Japanese birds. Estimated value: $20.00 to $30.00.*

PLATE 216. *Hummingbird on a leaf. Height 5½". Unmarked. Estimated value: $20.00 to $25.00.*

PLATE 217. *Bird with flowers. Height 6½". Mark: impressed* Made in Japan. *Estimated value: $20.00 to $25.00.*

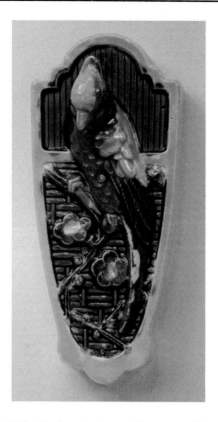

PLATE 218. Bird and cherry blossoms. Height 7½". Mark: circular impressed Made in Japan. The bird on this pocket projects out into space from the pocket. Estimated value: $20.00 to $25.00.

PLATE 219. Owl with lantern. Height 8½". Mark: ink stamp Made in Japan. This rather comical little owl is something of a departure from traditional bird pockets. Estimated value: $25.00 to $35.00.

PLATE 220. Three ducks. Height 5" x 5" wide. Mark: brown ink stamp Made in Japan. Note the two holes in the uplifted wings. Estimated value: $15.00 to $20.00 each.

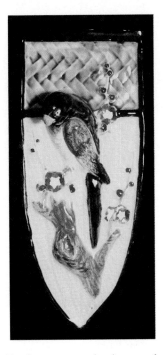

PLATE 221. Bird on woven background. Height 7½". Mark: impressed Made in Japan. Estimated value: $20.00 to $25.00.

PLATE 222. Bird on grape vine. Height 7¼". Mark: ink stamp Made in Japan. Note that some of the glaze on this bird and the leaves were airbrushed while other glaze was hand applied. Estimated value: $20.00 to $30.00.

PLATE 223. Parakeet in a tree. Height 7". Marked: red ink stamp Made in Japan. Estimated value: $15.00 to $20.00.

PLATE 224. Swan in lily pads. Height 6½". Mark: ink stamp Made in Japan. This pocket could be free standing in addition to hanging on the wall. Estimated value: $15.00 to $20.00.

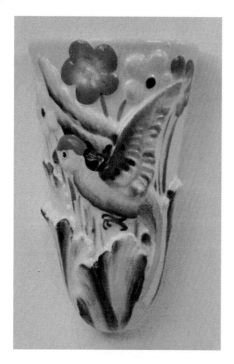

*PLATE 225. Parakeet in flight. Height unknown. Mark: ink stamp Made in Japan. Estimated value: $15.00 to $20.00.*

*PLATE 226. Two birds. Height 6". mark: ink stamp Hand Paint Made in Japan. Estimated value: $15.00 to $20.00.*

*PLATE 227. Blue bird on a basket. Height 8¼". Unmarked. Estimated value: $20.00 to $25.00.*

*PLATE 228. Large-billed bird. Height 8". Mark: ink stamp Made in Japan. This pocket is reminiscent in color and style to PLATE 219. Estimated value: $25.00 to $35.00.*

PLATE 229. *Parakeet on basket weave pocket. Height 7¼". Mark: ink stamp* Made in Japan. *Estimated value: $25.00 to $35.00.*

PLATE 230. *Parrot on a swing. Height 5½". Mark: ink stamp* Made in Occupied Japan. *The mark indicates that this pocket was made in the years just following World War II. This is not actually a wall pocket and originally had a chain from which it was hung. Estimated value: $25.00 to $35.00.*

PLATE 231. *Green bird. Height 8". Mark: impressed* Made in Japan. *This is a rather plain pocket although it is decorated with gold luster. Estimated value: $20.00 to $25.00.*

*PLATES 232 & 233. Swan in cattails. Height for both, 6½". Mark: Left, red ink stamp and impressed* Made in Japan. *Right, ink stamp* Made in Japan. *These pockets appear to have been cast from the same mold but have different marks suggesting they were made by different companies. Estimated value: $15.00 to $20.00 each.*

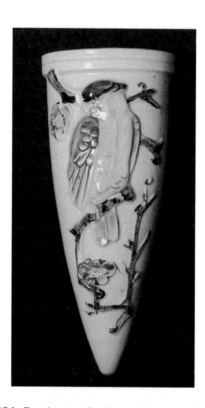 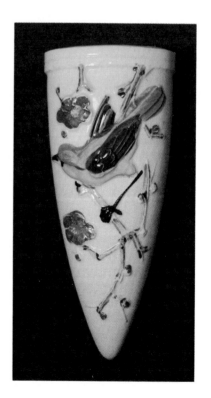

*PLATE 234. Parakeet with cherry blossoms. Height 7¼". Mark: ink stamp* Made in Japan. *A variety of this type of pocket can be found with various birds in various poses. They generally have a cream or slightly yellow body color and molded decoration. Estimated value: $15.00 to $20.00.*

*PLATE 235. Bird with cherry blossoms. Height 7". Mark: impressed* Made in Japan. *This is similar to PLATE 234. Estimated value: $15.00 to $20.00.*

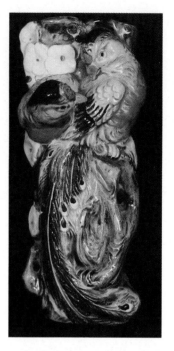

PLATE 236. Bird of Paradise with cherry blossoms. Height 7¼". Mark: ink stamp Made in Japan. This is another variation of PLATE 234. Estimated value: $15.00 to $20.00.

PLATE 237. Birds of Paradise. Height 8½". Mark: circular impressed Made in Japan. This is a lovely, three-dimensional pocket with good detail. Beginning with this pocket through PLATE 251, the pockets shown differ from most of the previous pockets in that they have light gray clay bodies and many of the glazes are translucent. Estimated value: $35.00 to $45.00.

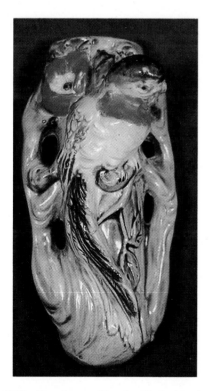

PLATE 238. Parakeet. Height 7¼". Mark: circular impressed Made in Japan. The head and shoulders of the bird project out from the pocket body. Estimated value: $20.00 to $30.00.

PLATE 239. Blue basket weave pocket with bird. Height 7½". Mark: impressed Made in Japan. The design on this pocket is in low relief and is fairly standard Japanese design. Estimated value: $20.00 to $30.00.

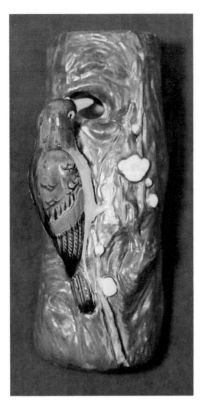

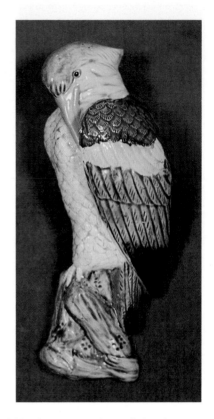

PLATE 240. *Woodpecker on a log. Height 7¼". Mark: impressed* Made in Japan. *The woodpecker's beak is poking into an open hole on this cleverly designed pocket. Estimated value: $25.00 to $35.00.*

PLATE 241. *Crane. Height 7½". Mark: impressed* Made in Japan. *This is a graceful Oriental design. Estimated value: $35.00 to $45.00.*

PLATE 242. *Bird of Paradise. Height 7½". Mark: impressed* Made in Japan. *Estimated value: $25.00 to $35.00.*

PLATE 243. *Duck in flight. Height 7" x 10¾" wide. Mark: impressed* Made in Japan. *Swooping out of the sky, this duck has beautifully molded details in the feathers. Estimated value: $35.00 to $45.00.*

PLATE 244. *Duck in flight. Height 4½" x 9½" wide. Mark: impressed* Made in Japan. *Not only is this pocket somewhat smaller than the previous one, but it is more crudely painted and the molded detail is not as clear. Estimated value: $30.00 to $40.00.*

PLATE 245. *Parakeet. Height 9". Mark: ink stamp* Made in Japan. *Estimated value: $30.00 to $40.00.*

PLATE 246. *Red headed bird. Height 7¼". Mark: ink stamp* Made in Japan. *Note how the head projects out into space from the rest of the pocket. Estimated value: $25.00 to $35.00.*

PLATE 247. *Parrot on a limb. Height 8". Mark: impressed* Made in Japan. *Estimated value: $20.00 to $30.00.*

PLATE 249. *Parakeet. Height 8". Mark: impressed* Made in Japan. *Estimated value: $20.00 to $30.00.*

PLATE 248. *Owl. Height 6". Mark: impressed* Made in Japan. *Looking more shocked than wise, the expression on this owl makes him an interesting addition to a collection. Estimated value: $20.00 to $30.00.*

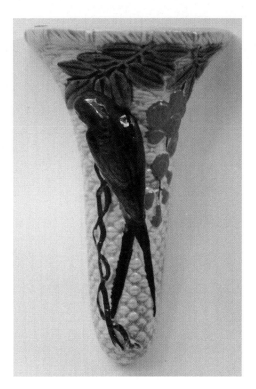

*PLATE 250. Crested cockatoo. Height 11¼". Mark: impressed Made in Japan. This is an unusually large and lovely Japanese bird. Estimated value: $35.00 to $45.00.*

*PLATE 251. Basket weave pocket with blue bird. Height unknown. Mark: impressed Made in Japan. Estimated value: $20.00 to $25.00.*

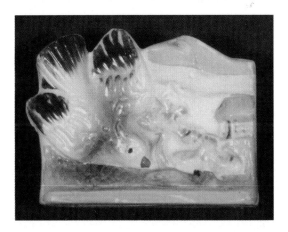

*PLATE 252. Bluebird with oriental scene. Height 2½" x 3½" wide. Mark: impressed Japan. This tiny pocket is one of a pair. The other has a red bird. Estimated value: $10.00 to $15.00.*

*PLATE 253. Birds on a book. Height 2½" x 3¼" wide. Mark: ink stamp Japan. Estimated value: $10.00 to $15.00.*

PLATE 254. Cuckoo clocks. Height excluding string and weights, large 7½", medium 5½", small 3½". Mark: ink stamp Made in Japan. This style of pocket may be one of the most common of all Japanese pockets. Variations of size, color, and time make each one unique. Some are decorated with flowers and some have grapes. Some are decorated with luster while others are not. Try to find the ones that still have their little pine cone clock weights. Estimated value: Large and medium, $15.00 to $25.00, small, $20.00 to $25.00.

Many Japanese wall pockets were decorated with lusters of various colors. Nowhere are lusters used to better advantage than in the decoration of bird wall pockets.

PLATE 255. Green bird on amber luster. Height 7". Mark: circular green ink stamp, Hand Painted, Made in Japan written around a flower. This is a very typical wall pocket shape, especially for those made in Japan. Estimated value: $25.00 to $35.00.

PLATE 256. Owl luster. Height 5¼". Unmarked. While unmarked, this pocket has several characteristics of Japanese pockets, the style of the flowers and the background colors among them. Estimated value: $20.00 to $25.00.

PLATE 257. Green parakeet with amber background. Height 6¼". Unmarked. Parakeets were popular design motifs on Japanese pockets. Estimated value: $20.00 to $30.00.

PLATE 258. White peacock. Height 6". Mark: ink stamp and impressed Made in Japan. Estimated value: $25.00 to $30.00.

PLATE 259. Blue crested bird on fruit. Height 6¾". Mark: circular red ink stamp Hand Painted, Made in Japan around a bird in flight. This is a beautifully decorated pocket in wonderful condition. Estimated value: $30.00 to $40.00.

PLATE 260. Mother bird with chicks. Height 7½". Mark: red ink stamp Hand Paint, Made in Japan. This pocket is similar to PLATE 197 but this time done in lusters. Estimated value: $30.00 to $35.00.

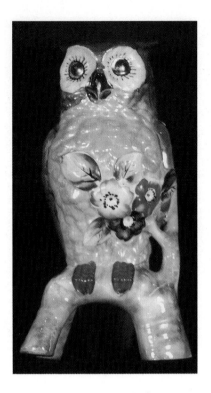

PLATE 261. Bluebird perched upside down. Height 9¼". Mark: circular green ink stamp Hand Paint, Made in Japan around a flower. This is an unusually large pocket with the bird in a rather unusual pose. Estimated value: $30.00 to $40.00.

PLATE 262. Large owl. Height 9½". Unmarked. This is another large pocket. This one can serve as a free standing planter and it has a hole to hang it on the wall. It is really a three-dimensional piece and looks rather awkward hung. Estimated value: $30.00 to $40.00.

PLATE 263. Canary with strawberries. Height 5¾". Mark: ink stamp Made in Japan. Estimated value: $20.00 to $25.00.

PLATE 264. Luster crane. Height 7¼". Mark: circular ink stamp Hand Paint, Made in Japan around interlocking diamonds with a "T" in each diamond. This pocket features careful hand painting. Notice how the blue fades from light to dark. His yellow chest is luster. Estimated value: $30.00 to $35.00.

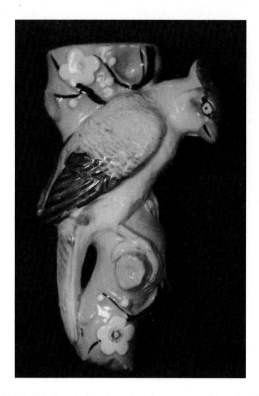

PLATE 265. Pink bird with blue crest. Height 7½". Mark: circular red ink stamp, Hand Painted, Made in Japan around a bird in flight. Estimated value: $25.00 to $35.00.

PLATE 266. Orange bird with crest. height 7½". Mark: ink stamp Hand Paint, Made in Japan. Also four impressed Japanese written characters. This is the author's only Japanese pocket with actual Japanese writing on it. It has a yellow luster background. Estimated value: $25.00 to $35.00.

PLATE 267. Yellow and gold luster bird. height 9¼". Mark: green ink stamp, Hand Paint, Made in Japan. This pocket is very similar to PLATES 265 and 266 but larger. All have yellow eyes lined in black that give them a rather irritated look that suggests they might peck your eyes out if they came to life! Estimated value: $30.00 to $40.00.

*PLATE 268 & 269. Green parakeet with amber luster background. Height 5½". Mark: circular red ink stamp, Hand Paint, Made in Japan around interlocking diamonds with a "T" inside each diamond. This pocket is rather unique in that its sides were beveled to fit into a corner (right pocket). It is one of only a few pockets known to the author to fit in corners including PLATE 270 and a Roseville pocket. Estimated value: $35.00 to $45.00.*

*PLATE 270. Red bird in blue oval. Height 8¼". Mark: circular red ink stamp Gold Castle, Hand Painted, Made in Japan around a red Japanese style castle. This narrow, tapered pocket also fits into a corner. Its beveled sides are also lustered, however, suggesting that it was also designed to hang on a flat wall. Estimated value: $30.00 to $35.00.*

PLATE 271. *Yellow bird. Height 9". Mark: circular black ink stamp,* Hand Paint, Made in Japan *around a flower shape. This is an unusually large luster pocket. The two birds were attached to the basic pocket before it was bisque fired. The three-dimensional quality of the design and the careful decoration make it valuable. Estimated value: $35.00 to $50.00.*

PLATE 272. *Yellow bird with pink crest. Height 7½". Mark: ink stamp,* Made in Japan. *Estimated value: $25.00 to $35.00.*

PLATE 273. Three luster bird pockets. Left, yellow tufted bird. Height 5". Mark: circular ink stamp, Hand Painted, Made in Japan around a bird in flight. Middle, blue bird with red wing. Mark: same mark as first pocket. Right, blue and green bird. Height 5". Mark: circular red ink stamp, Hand Painted, Made in Japan around a flower. These are typical examples of Japanese bird pockets. Birds are often portrayed perched on a tree limb. Japanese decorators did not seem to concern themselves with accurate colorations of actual birds in the wild and tended to use various combinations of bright colors with luster. Estimated value of each: $25.00 to $35.00.

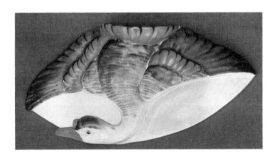

PLATE 274. Goose in flight. Height 5½" x 8" wide. Mark: circular red ink stamp Hand Painted, Made in Japan around a flower. This in an unusual shape with excellent hand-painted detail accented with luster. Estimated value: $35.00 to $45.00.

PLATE 275. Parrot. Height 7". Unmarked. This beautiful pocket has typical Japanese luster colors and outstanding design. The parrot's head and upper body extends out into space from the basic vase shape of the pocket. Estimated value: $35.00 to $45.00.

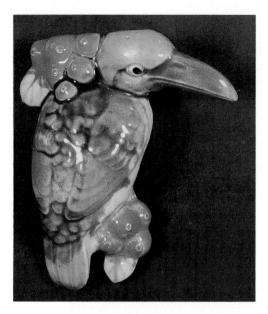

*PLATES 276 & 277. Macaw. Height 5½". Mark: ink stamp Made in Japan. The left figure has a porcelain body and is decorated with china paint and luster. The right figure has a white clay body and glazed decoration. They both appear to be the same design. Estimated value: $20.00 to $30.00 each.*

People are also portrayed in Japanese wall pockets. Children and adults are both seen and they often have a distinctly Caucasian look that suggests that they were designed for the United States export market.

*PLATE 278. 18th century man and woman. Height 6". Mark: red ink stamp, Made in Occupied Japan. After World War II until 1952, wares imported from Japan into this country were marked "Made in Occupied Japan." Occupied Japan wares constitute a whole area of collecting for some and the prices are generally higher than for objects without the "Occupied" designation. This lovely bisque double pocket was probably designed as a match holder or perhaps for toothpicks. Estimated value: $55.00.*

*PLATE 279. Dutch girl carrying a basket. Height 5½". Mark: ink stamp and impressed mark Made in Japan. This is an interesting design not often seen. Estimated value: $25.00 to $35.00.*

PLATE 280. *18th century woman. Height 6½". Mark: ink stamp Made in Japan. Estimated value: $20.00 to $25.00.*

PLATE 281. *Boy holding up basket. Height 6¾". Mark: red ink stamp Made in Japan. This pocket can be found in a variety of color combinations. Estimated value: $20.00 to $25.00.*

PLATE 282. *Boy feeding a rabbit. Height 6¼". Mark: ink stamp Made in Japan. This is a sweet scene and would look nice in a child's room. Estimated value: $20.00 to $30.00.*

PLATE 283. *Girl reading. Height 5½". Mark: red ink* stamp Made in Japan. *The Japanese produced a variety of pockets depicting children that looked somewhat like Hummel designs. Estimated value: $20.00 to $25.00.*

PLATE 284. *Boy on a fence. Height 5". Mark: red ink* stamp Japan. *This pocket looks like it might be a mate to PLATE 283 but they are different heights and widths. Estimated value: $20.00 to $25.00.*

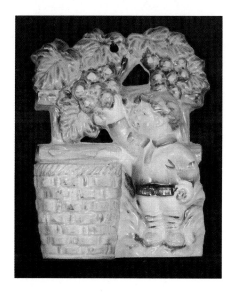

PLATE 285. *Boy with grapes. Height 5⅛". Mark: ink* stamp Japan. *Here is another Hummel-like figure that was probably meant to be a match holder. Estimated value: $20.00 to $25.00.*

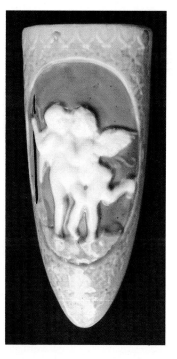

PLATE 286. *Cherubs kissing. Height 6¾". Mark: ink* stamp and impressed Made in Japan. *This pocket is sometimes found in other color combinations. It is rather crudely decorated but the in-mold design in the pink background is nicely detailed. Estimated value: $15.00 to $20.00.*

PLATE 288. Boy with tie. Height 4½". Mark: ink stamp Japan. *I have only seen this little pocket once. Estimated value: $25.00 to $35.00.*

PLATE 287. Dancing woman. Height 8". Mark: red ink stamp Made in Japan. *This beautiful deco style pocket fits so close to the wall that it looks like a wall plaque. However, there is a pocket opening behind her shoulders. The airbrushed design on the skirt is unusual. Estimated value: $35.00 to $45.00.*

PLATE 289. Girl with blue hat. Height 2". Mark: circular red ink stamp, Quality Guaranteed, Japan. *A variety of women's faces in different hats were made by this company. The faces are usually carefully painted and they are often quite small although occasionally larger sizes will be found. Estimated value: $20.00 to $25.00.*

PLATE 290. Girl in black hat. Height 3". Mark: circular red ink stamp, Quality Guaranteed, Japan. *This pocket is somewhat larger than the previous pocket but was made by the same company. Estimated value: $20.00 to $25.00.*

PLATE 291. Girl in light blue hat. Height 3". Mark: circular red ink stamp, Quality Guaranteed, Japan. *Estimated value: $20.00 to $25.00.*

*PLATE 292. Girl in yellow hat. Height 3". Mark: circular red ink stamp,* Quality Guaranteed, Japan. *Estimated value: $20.00 to $25.00.*

*PLATE 293. Boy under tree. Height 4⅛". Mark: red ink stamp,* Japan. *Estimated value: $10.00 to $15.00.*

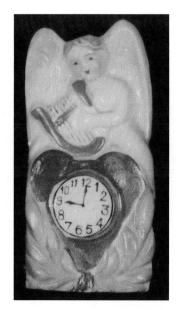

*PLATE 294. Cherub with a clock. Height 4". Mark: ink stamp* Made in Japan. *This little pocket originally had string and clock weights that hung from the bottom. Estimated value: without clock weights, $5.00 to $10.00.*

*PLATE 295. Girl in blue hat. Height 3". Mark: impressed* Japan. *Estimated value: $10.00 to $15.00.*

PLATE 296. Spanish dancer. Height 6". Mark: ink stamp Made in Japan. Deco style dancers can be found from time to time. Estimated value: $25.00 to $35.00.

Fruits and flowers are often seen in Japanese wall pockets.

PLATE 297. Fruit in blue basket. Height approximately 8". Mark: ink stamp Made in Japan. Baskets with their handles still intact are a find. When buying a basket pocket without a handle, be sure and check that the handle was not broken off and the remains ground down. Estimated value: $20.00 to $25.00.

PLATE 298. Berries and leaves. Height 12". Mark: black ink stamp Made in Japan. This is an unusually large pocket with good modeling and detail. Estimated value: $25.00 to $35.00.

PLATE 299. Yellow and pink tulips. Height approximately 7". Mark: impressed Made in Japan. Estimated value: $20.00 to $25.00.

PLATE 300. Blue luster with cherry blossoms. Height 6". Mark: circular ink stamp Japan-Mitsu-Insos around three stars. Cherry blossoms are seen often on Japanese pockets. Estimated value: $15.00 to $20.00.

PLATE 301. Amber luster with cherry blossoms. Height 6". Mark: ink stamp Made in Japan. This pocket looks almost identical to PLATE 299 but the mark is different and, besides the background color, there are slight differences in the execution of the design which is typical of hand decoration. Estimated value: $15.00 to $20.00.

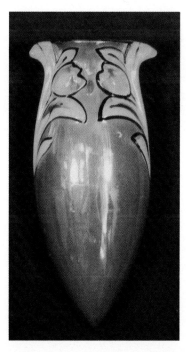

PLATE 302. Blue luster with pink tulips. Height: 5¼". Mark: circular red ink stamp Made in Japan around a bird. This pocket also bears a foil label that reads "Souvenir of Bastrop, Texas." Estimated value: $10.00 to $15.00.

PLATE 303. Orange pocket with flowers. Height 7½". Mark: Gold Castle, Handpainted, Chikusa, Made in Japan. While the shape is simple, the handpainting is careful and very lovely. Estimated value: $25.00 to $35.00.

PLATE 304. Basket with fruit and flower decoration. Height 8". Mark: impressed Made in Japan. This has the grayish clay body sometimes used with this type of glazing. Estimated value: $20.00 to $30.00.

PLATE 305. Yellow basket weave with handles. Height 6¼". Mark: ink stamp Made in Japan. Estimated value: $20.00 to $25.00.

PLATE 306. Blue basket weave. Height 6". Mark: impressed Made in Japan. Pockets like this and PLATE 303 are fairly common. Estimated value: $20.00 to $25.00.

PLATE 307. *Blue with Shasta daisies. Height 8". Mark: impressed* Made in Japan. *This rather large pocket has a grayish clay body and translucent glaze colors. These types of pockets (PLATES 302, 303, and 304 also) are sometimes described as "Japanese majolica," a misnomer since no majolica was produced in Japan. Estimated value: $20.00 to $25.00.*

PLATE 308. *Red Peony. Height 8". Mark: impressed* Made in Japan. *This graceful design is sometimes found in other color combinations. Estimated value: $20.00 to $30.00.*

PLATE 309. *Yellow basket with flowers. Height 6¼". Mark: impressed* Made in Japan. *This is an interesting design with some reticulation (cut outs). Notice the air-brushed shading on the rose. Estimated value: $20.00 to $25.00.*

PLATE 310. *Pocket on plaque with birds. Height 8¼". Mark: impressed* Made in Japan. *Estimated value: $20.00 to $25.00.*

This next section of pictures demonstrates the variety of design inspirations the Japanese drew from. Sailboats are not uncommon in wall pockets. Abstract deco designs were also popular in the twenties.

*PLATE 311. Spanish galleon. Height 7". Mark: circular red ink stamp* Hand Paint, Made in Japan *around interlocking diamonds with a "T" in each diamond. This beautifully detailed and colorful sailboat is a wonderful addition to any collection. Estimated value: $30.00 to $40.00.*

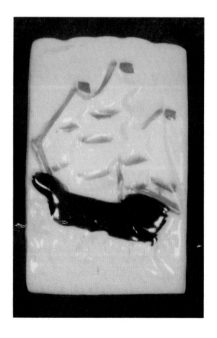

*PLATE 312. Sailboat. height 3½". Mark: ink stamp* Made in Japan. *Estimated value: $10.00 to $15.00.*

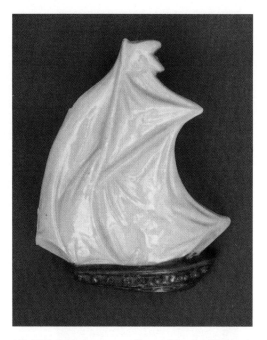

PLATE 313. Luster sailboat. Height 5". Mark: impressed Japan. Careful sculpting of the sails gives this little pocket a nice, three-dimensional quality. Estimated value: $20.00 to $25.00.

PLATE 314. Windmill scene. Height 7". Mark: ink stamp Made in Japan. This is an interesting, hand-decorated scene. Estimated value: $20.00 to $25.00.

PLATE 315. Niagara Falls. Height 7¼". Mark: red ink stamp of maple leaf, Famous Parkdale Novelty, Hand Painted, Japan written within the leaf. This pocket was produced specifically as a souvenir of a trip to the Canadian side of Niagara Falls. It is remarkable because of its very detailed, hand-painted picture executed in china paint. The amount of hand work on this pocket produced as an inexpensive souvenir suggests how cheap skilled labor was in Japan. Estimated value: $35.00 to $45.00.

PLATE 316. Deco luster pocket. Height 8½". Mark: amber luster stamp Made in Japan. This pocket belonged to my mother and hung in our home throughout my childhood. It was my first introduction into the wonderful world of wall pockets. Estimated value: to me, priceless; to everyone else, $30.00 to $40.00.

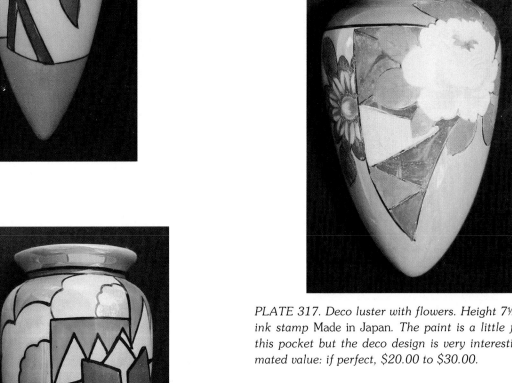

PLATE 317. Deco luster with flowers. Height 7½". Mark: ink stamp Made in Japan. The paint is a little faded on this pocket but the deco design is very interesting. Estimated value: if perfect, $20.00 to $30.00.

PLATE 318. Abstract deco pocket. Height 7½". Mark: circular ink stamp Gold Castle, Hand Painted, Made in Japan around a Japanese pagoda. This is a great deco design with beautiful lusters and colors. Estimated value: $35.00 to $45.00.

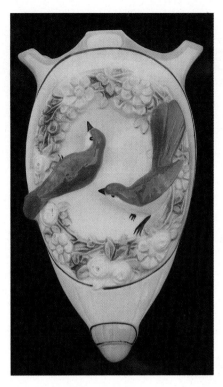

PLATE 319. Blue Birds. Height approximately 8½".
Mark: ink stamp Made in Japan. Estimated value: $20.00
to $30.00.

The Japanese depicted a variety of domestic and wild animals in their pockets.

PLATE 321. Palomino horse head. Height 3½". Mark:
ink stamp Made in Japan. Estimated value: $5.00 to
$10.00.

PLATE 320. Horse head in a horseshoe. Height 5".
Mark: ink stamp Made in Japan. Estimated value: $5.00
to $10.00.

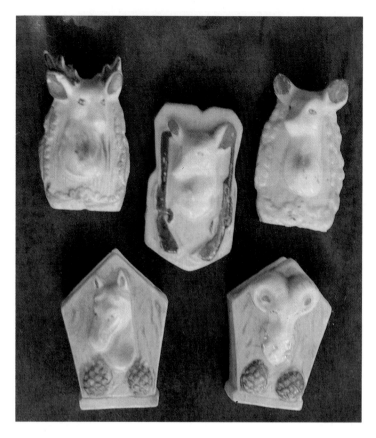

PLATE 322. Miniature trophy heads. Height 3 to 3¼". Marks: ink stamp Japan. Animal heads seem a rather odd design choice for such tiny wall pockets unless they were to be marketed to children. I have not encountered larger versions. The horse head is particularly bizarre since the only stuffed horse I know of is Roy Roger's Trigger (well, I heard he stuffed him). Estimated value: $15.00 to $20.00.

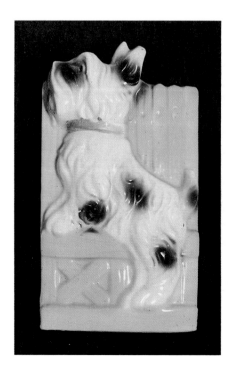

PLATE 323 (left). Scotty by a fence. Height 5½". Mark: red ink stamp and impressed Made in Japan. Scotty dogs were popular during the 1920s and they were often used as design elements during that period. They are popular collectibles now. Estimated value: $15.00 to $20.00.

PLATE 324 (right). Luster elephant. Height 7". Mark: ink stamp Made in Japan. This is a very unusual pocket with the animal represented as though the rest of his body is inside the wall. This particular pocket was pictured in a Noritake catalog and was originally sold for $3.75 per dozen. Estimated value: $35.00 to $45.00.

Some Japanese pockets actually look Japanese and some may have been produced for the domestic market in that country. Graceful men and women in native costumes can often be found. Pockets that are decorated in traditional Japanese arts and crafts style are especially interesting and evocative of Japan.

*PLATE 325. Japanese man. Height 9½". Mark: impressed* Made in Japan, *also impressed Japanese character writing. Produced in a grayish white clay, the faces and hands on this type of pocket are often left unglazed and the costume colorfully glazed. Estimated value: $60.00 to $75.00.*

*PLATE 326. Japanese woman with fan. Height 9". Mark: impressed* Made in Japan. *Found seperately, this pocket looks like it might be a pair to PLATE 325. Dealer price: $110.00.*

PLATE 327. *Japanese man with basket. Height 8".* Unmarked, but I have seen others impressed and ink stamped. This style along with its mate (PLATE 328) are the most commonly found Japanese figurals. These traditionally dressed male and female pockets seem to be rising rapidly in price. *Estimated value: $60.00 to $75.00.*

PLATE 328. *Japanese woman with basket. Height 8½".* Mark: impressed *Made in Japan.* See discussion of PLATE 325. *Estimated value: $60.00 to $75.00.*

PLATE 329. *Japanese character. Height 7".* Unmarked. This is a rather rare wall pocket. The fact that it is unmarked suggests that it may have been made for the domestic Japanese market rather than for export. It may have also had a paper label that has come off, however. *Estimated value: $45.00 to $60.00.*

PLATE 330. Luster pocket with scene. Height 6¼". Mark: ink stamp Made in Japan. Variations of this placid scene appear on all sorts of Japanese luster ware. Tea sets, vases, cake plates, and ashtrays all can be found with the calm Oriental scene hand painted on it. Estimated value: $25.00 to $35.00.

PLATE 331. Iris wall pocket. Height 11¾". Unmarked. The petals of the iris are applied clay with glaze over it to give a three-dimensional quality. There are also flower decorations on each side. Estimated value: $35.00 to $45.00.

PLATE 332. Brown Satsuma pocket. Height 8". Mark: circular orange ink stamp Hand Painted, Japan around a flower, 2748 beneath the mark. Raised slip decoration and gold accents highlight this desirable Satsuma style pocket with traditional Japanese decoration. Estimated value: $35.00 to $45.00.

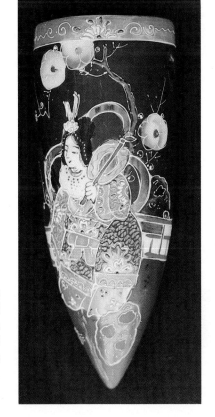

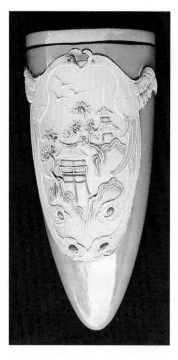

PLATE 333. *Moriage and luster pocket. height 6¾". Mark: circular red ink stamp* Hand Painted, Made in Japan *around three stylized plants. Moriage decoration is achieved with raised slip decoration. This is a traditional design with a large bird on each side of an Oriental scene with temples and trees. Estimated value: $35.00 to $45.00.*

PLATE 334. *Dragonware pocket. Height 7¼". Unmarked. This piece is part of a broad line of wares from Japan that feature an undulating dragon accented by raised slip decoration and gold luster. It is sometimes referred to as Gray Dragonware. Estimated value: $35.00 to $45.00.*

PLATE 335. *Flowers with raised glaze decoration. Height 8½". Mark: red ink stamp* Made in Japan. *The raised glaze decoration is much like that found on* PLATE 332. *This pocket is sometimes found with a green background as well as the blue background shown. Estimated value: $30.00 to $45.00.*

PLATE 336. *Oriental teapot. Height unknown. Mark: impressed* Made in Japan. *This little teapot had a metal handle originally. Estimated value: $10.00 to $15.00.*

The following are a type of pocket produced in Japan with a rather heavy clay body and cold painted decoration. They frequently have black backgrounds but come in other colors as well. They generally have an Oriental design motif and most have an impressed "Made in Japan" mark. The black ones with textured background were meant to imitate a more expensive type of Japanese ware known as "bark cloisonné." These pockets tend to be fairly inexpensive but have a faithful following of collectors.

*PLATE 337. Black pocket with daisy. Height 7½". Mark: circular impressed* Made in Japan. *This is a typical black pocket with a colored design on a black background with gold accents. Estimated value: $15.00 to $20.00.*

*PLATE 338. Black pocket with gold. Height 9". Mark: impressed* Made in Japan. *The molded design is accented with gold paint. Estimated value: $20.00 to $30.00.*

PLATE 339. *Yellow flowers on orange background. Height 7". Mark: circular impressed* Made in Japan. *Estimated value: $20.00 to $25.00.*

PLATE 340. *Yellow flower on black. Height 10". Mark: impressed* Made in Japan. *This very large pocket has a beautiful Oriental design molded into it. Estimated value: $25.00 to $35.00.*

PLATE 341. *Fruit on black. Height 9". Mark: impressed* Made in Japan. *Estimated value: with damage to paint on fruit, $15.00 to $20.00.*

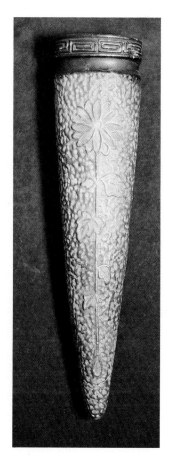

PLATE 342. Black dragon. Height 7". Mark: impressed Made in Japan. Estimated value: $15.00 to $20.00.

PLATE 343. Blue daisy on textured background. Height 7". Mark: impressed Made in Japan. This pocket and the one pictured in PLATE 338 are very similar in shape. Estimated value: $15.00 to $20.00.

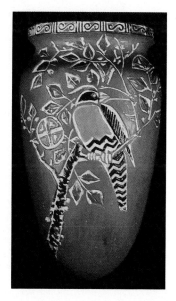

PLATE 344. Orange pocket with bird. Height 7". Mark: impressed Made in Japan. This pocket has a nice, stylized, Oriental design. Estimated value: $20.00 to $25.00.

PLATE 345. *Turquoise pocket with stylized flower. Height 8¼". Mark: impressed* Made in Japan. *Estimated value: $15.00 to $20.00.*

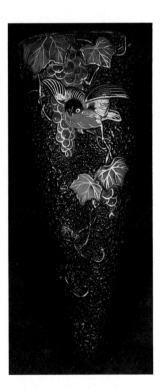

PLATE 346. *Red pocket with lily. Height 9¼". Mark: impressed* Made in Japan. *Estimated value: $15.00 to $20.00.*

PLATE 347. *Black bark cloisonné with bird. Height 9". Mark: impressed* Made in Japan. *This type of pocket is often found with flaking paint. This particular one is in excellent condition with even the gold detail still shiny. Estimated value: $25.00 to $35.00.*

# Majolica

Majolica may well be the quintessential pottery of the Victorian era. With its beautiful colors and many styles, it captures the opulence, extravagance, and ornate nature of that time. According to Marilyn Karmason, an authority on majolica, "The most engaging aspects of Victorian majolica are its humor, whimsy, charm, elegance, and great natural beauty."

Majolica was first produced in England during the Victorian era by the Minton Company. It was unveiled to the public at the Crystal Palace Exhibit (formally titled London's Great Exhibition of the Works of Industry of All Nations), an extravagant event that was promoted by Queen Victoria's beloved Prince Albert. Majolica was an instant success and it was soon copied and produced by many potteries both great and small, first in England and then in America and on the continent of Europe.

A wide variety of dinnerwares as well as decorative items for the home were produced in the colorful majolica. Among the decorative items produced were wall pockets. Victorians were very interested in horticulture and liked to bring their gardens indoors as much as possible. Majolica provided a colorful, often naturalistic way to do this.

Majolica continued to be popular throughout the Victorian era. While its production had died out by the turn of the century in England and America, it continued to be produced on the continent of Europe into the 1920s.

Today, majolica is a highly sought after and expensive collectible. Like many expensive wares, it has its imitators. I am not aware of any majolica wall pocket reproductions but the collector should be on guard. Most reproduction majolica feels lighter than old majolica and the quality reproductions are marked as such. Any wall pocket made in Japan is not majolica.

Those wall pocket collectors who are lucky enough to have a majolica wall pocket included in their collection indeed have a treasure.

PLATE 348. Majolica basket weave with ivy. Height: 8¾". Mark: rosette of four "W"s with a "C" in the center and a crown above. Made by Worcester Royal Porcelain Works (now known as the Royal Worcester Porcelain Company Ltd.) in England. Produced in the 1880s. Estimated value: $400.00 to $595.00.

PLATE 349. Majolica hat. Height 7". Unmarked but probably made in England around 1880. Hats are a fairly popular wall pocket design motif. A new wall pocket is currently in production that is quite similar to this one. Estimated value: $325.00 to $495.00.

PLATE 350. Majolica cocketiel. Height 15" x 10" wide. Mark: Holdcroft. This beautiful wall pocket was made by Joseph Holdcroft, a well-known English majolica maker during the 1880s. It has great detail and lustrous colors. The eyes are made of glass and were installed after glaze firing. Estimated value: $1,500.00.

PLATE 351. *Turquoise basket weave with leaves. Height 5". Unmarked but judged by the dealer to be either American or English from the 1880s. Estimated value: $175.00 to $250.00.*

PLATE 352. *Sanded wall pocket with turquoise ribbon handle. Height 6½". This is unmarked, as much majolica is, but it is probably from England and made in the 1880s. Fine sand was sometimes sprinkled on the wet glazed surface of majolica wares and then fired. The result is a surface of interesting texture as seen on this yellow background and the reddish brown stems of the applied roses and leaves. Estimated value: $250.00 to $375.00.*

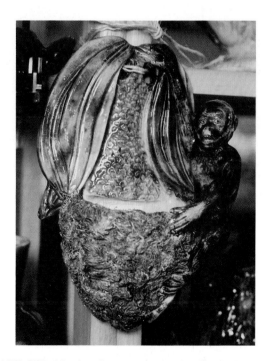

PLATE 353. *Monkey by a nest. Height 8". Mark:* Sousza, Portugal. *Portugal, like other European countries, produced interesting majolica. Note the applied, clay texture added to the basket. The wall pocket has more of a hand-made look rather than cast from a mold. Much of Portugal's majolica has a rustic, handmade look with much applied decoration. This wall pocket was probably made around 1890. Estimated value: $700.00 to $895.00.*

PLATE 354. *Small basket weave match safe with leaves and butterfly. Height 4". Unmarked but identified by the dealer as Portuguese and made around 1880. Estimated value: $200.00 to $300.00.*

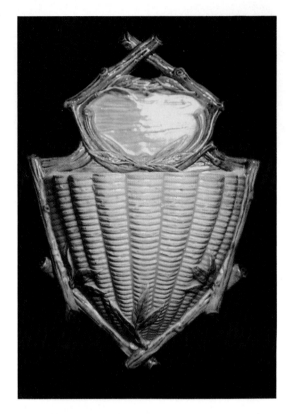

PLATE 355. Leaf wall pocket with bird perched on a branch. Height 12". Mark: four "W"s with a "C" in the middle. Made by the Worcester Porcelain Works. This large, interesting pocket is a good example of the naturalistic design often seen in majolica. This pocket was made in England around 1880. Estimated value: $500.00 to $650.00.

PLATE 356. Basket weave and twig pocket. Height 10". Mark: GJ. George Jones was a famous maker of majolica in England. His wares are highly sought after for their interesting, well executed designs and their beautiful colors. Turquoise is often a dominant color in his designs. This pocket also dates from about 1880. Estimated value: $1,200.00.

PLATE 357. Sanded shell with rope handle and applied flowers. Height 10½". Unmarked. The applied flowers and yellow sanded background on this pocket are quite similar to PLATE 352. This pocket is also probably from England. Estimated value: $325.00 to $450.00.

# Glass Wall Pockets

Glass wall pockets were first produced in the Pittsburgh area around 1876. These pockets were used as match safes to be hung beside the stove or fireplace. Washington Beck, who was associated with several glass works in the Pittsburgh area, took out a patent for a glass wall pocket representing Columbia, a classical woman often used to represent the United States during that time. He also patented a variation featuring a jester's head with cap and bells. Small wall pockets for use as match safes were also imported from England during that time. The English versions generally can be distinguished from the American pockets by a design registry mark on the back. This mark consists of a diamond shape with letters and numbers impressed into the glass.

American companies who produced decorative glasswares made a variety of wall pockets to complement their other lines. Some of the better known manufacturers of glass wall pockets were the U.S. Glass Company, the Westmoreland Glass Company, and the Fostoria Glass Company.

During the Depression, a wide variety of inexpensive glassware was produced. This glassware was sold through variety stores, catalogs, and given away as premiums with other products. The U.S. Glass Company, a maker of what is now called Depression glass, produced several glass wall pockets which they referred to as wall vases. Their ads clearly imply that the wall vases were designed to hold cut flowers. In an ad that pictured a wall pocket and a car bud vase, they boasted that "from the daintiest bud, nestling alone, to the largest fully-developed bloom, in masses, there is some suitable receptacle in our varied lines." Their line included carnival glass pockets and clear glass pockets.

The U.S. Glass Company was a large conglomerate of factories. In 1891 they bought the A.J. Beatty and Sons glassworks in Tiffin, Ohio, know as the Tiffin Glass Company. The U.S. Glass Company referred to this plant as Factory R. Tiffin continued to make their own line of glass products which were considered to be of high quality. The Tiffin factory did not advertise as a

separate line and their products were often incorporated into catalogs of the U.S. Glass Company. Tiffin made a number of lovely glass wall pockets. Some were plain satin glass and others had the addition of hand cold painting or etching. For the collector, there is often confusion in identifying Tiffin Glass versus U.S. Glass.

The Jeanette Glass Company also produced Depression glass. Although produced after the Depression in 1947, their Anniversary line included a wall pocket. Number 1930 was described as a "pin-up vase" in their catalog. This pattern was produced in crystal and iridescent. The line was made until 1972, although it is not known if the wall pocket was made for that long.

The only glass pockets that have been seen by the author that might be classified as carnival glass have all been in the marigold color. A wall pocket and a car vase are both pictured in *The Collectors Encyclopedia of Carnival Glass* by Sherman Hand.

The Westmoreland Glass Company, well know for its carnival glass, also produced glass wall pockets in several colors.

The Fostoria Glass Company, one of the largest manufacturers of handmade glassware in the world, made wall pockets during their first 50 years of operation. Fostoria introduced color into its lines in 1924. Between that time and 1929, the company produced two wall pockets. Number 1881 was produced in crystal and ebony. Number 1681 was offered in amber, blue, green, crystal, and ebony.

The Dugan/Diamond Glass Company was in business from 1891 until 1931, when a fire destroyed the plant. Few lines from this company have been identified. It is known that Dugan/Diamond made two carnival glass pockets in marigold. One features a bird with grapes and one features a woodpecker. These pockets were apparently also made in other colors besides the iridescent marigold.

The Imperial Glass Company, famous for carnival glass and later, their Candlewick line, also produced carnival glass wall pockets as well as car vases.

A catalog from around 1938 for the Mantle Lamp Company of America who made the familiar Aladdin lamp, shows what appears to be glass wall pockets. These were made in their Alacite line, an ivory toned, translucent glass with fiery undertones when held to light.

Prices for glass wall pockets are somewhat difficult to ascertain. They were generally produced as a novelty item by most manufacturers and they are referred to only in passing by most authorities on glassware. They are not often listed in price guides and prices on the market seem to vary widely. A collector may find one color of a particular pocket for $20.00 and another color for $60.00. This variation does not appear to be related to the rarity of the color or style but merely differences in pricing by dealers.

*PLATES 358, 359, 360 & 361. Woodpecker wall pocket. Height 8½" x 1¾" wide. Made by the Dugan/Diamond Glass Company during the 1920s. Black seems to be the most frequently seen color and pink the rarest. Estimated value: $45.00 to $55.00 each.*

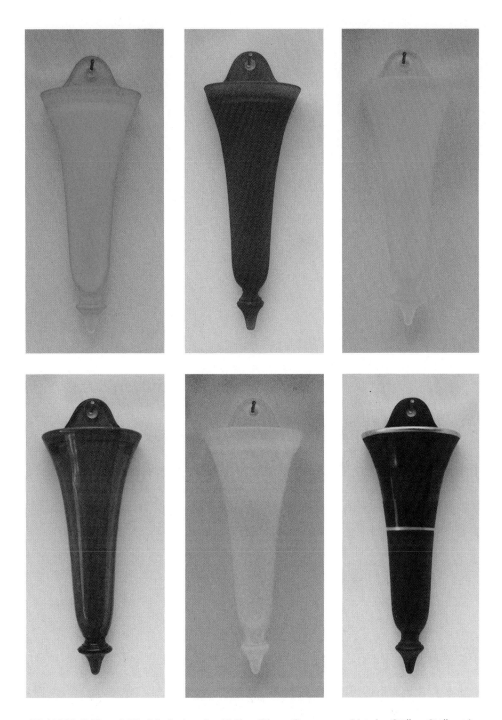

*PLATES 362 – 367. Made by the Tiffin Glass Company. Height 9½" x 3⅜" wide. PLATE 362 is light blue with a satin finish. PLATE 363 is teal colored with aqua bands and has a satin finish. PLATE 364 is green with a satin finish. PLATE 365 is red with a clear finish. PLATE 366 is canary yellow with a satin finish. PLATE 367 is shiny opaque black with applied gold bands which Tiffin called their Echel Finish. The Echel line used various colors and had both satin and shiny finishes but all were decorated with gold bands. Estimated value: $50.00 to $75.00 each. Red: $100.00.*

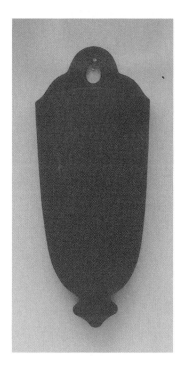

*PLATES 368, 369 & 370. Made by the Tiffin Glass Company. Height 9¼" x 3⅞" wide. PLATE 368 is amethyst with a satin finish, PLATE 369 is amber with a satin finish, PLATE 370 is light blue with a satin finish. This pocket was also produced in jasper, canary, royal blue, and black. Estimated value: $95.00 to $120.00 each.*

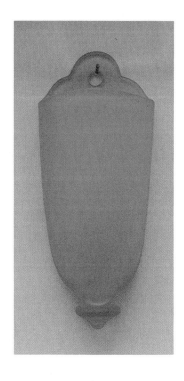

130

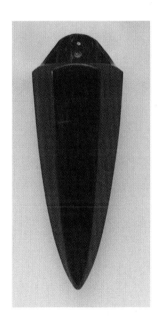
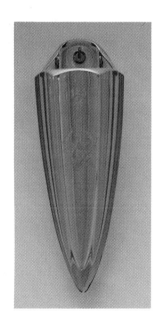

PLATES 371 – 375. Made by Fostoria. Height 8¼" x 3" wide. PLATE 371 is clear. PLATE 372 is amber with silver overlay decoration. PLATE 373 is black. PLATE 374 is green with silver overlay decoration. PLATE 375 is green with a gold Masonic symbol etched into the glass. Estimated value: $95.00 to $125.00 each.

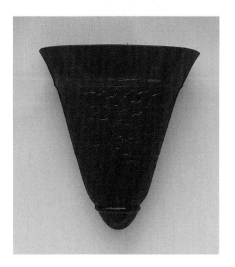 

*PLATES 376 – 379. Possibly made by U.S. Glass Company. Height 5⅞" x 5⅜" wide. PLATE 376 is black with a crackle finish. PLATE 377 is marigold with a crackle finish. PLATE 378 is black with vertical reeding. PLATE 379 is marigold with vertical reeding. These two styles are probably the most commonly found glass wall pockets on the market. The style with vertical reeding also came in clear. Black is seen less often than the marigold finish. The clear with vertical reeding is also sometimes found with cold painted decoration although it is not certain whether this was factory decoration or applied later. Estimated value: $25.00 to $35.00 for marigold; $30.00 to $40.00 for the black.*

PLATE 380. Made by the U.S. Glass Company. Height 6" x 5" wide. Shown here is white milk glass, a 1927 catalog of the company indicates that this pocket was also made in blue, green, and canary. It was also made in a satin finish. Estimated value: $40.00 to $50.00.

PLATE 381. Crystal wall pocket by the Jeannette Glass Company. Height 6½" x 3½" wide. This pocket was referred to by the company as a "pin-up vase." In addition to crystal, it was produced in a marigold iridescent and pink. This line, called Anniversary by the company, was produced as late as 1972. Estimated value: clear $15.00 to $20.00, colored $25.00 to $35.00.

PLATE 382. Green with white flowers. Height 6¾" x 4⅜" wide. Maker unknown. This may be Czechoslovakian. Unlike the American glass pockets, this one is hand blown and hand decorated. Estimated value: $40.00 to $50.00.

PLATE 383 & 384. Bird with grapes in clear and marigold. Height 7¾" x 7½" wide. Made by the Dugan/Diamond Glass Company. Estimated value: $35.00 to $45.00.

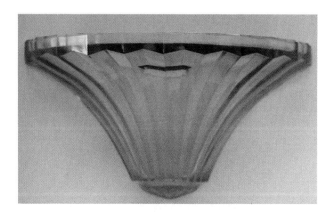

PLATE 385. Marigold wide mouthed pocket. Height 5½" x 10½" wide. Maker unknown. The sweeping shape of this pocket is very suggestive of the art deco period. Estimated value: $35.00 to $45.00.

PLATE 386. Orange cased glass pocket. Height 5¾" x 4½" wide. Maker unknown. This pocket has a white interior and back and on the outside swirled orange glass and black striped on the ridges. This pocket is unlike American-made pockets and is probably Czechoslovakian. Estimated value: $40.00 to $50.00.

*PLATE 387. Aqua blue violin. Height of bottle 10".
Maker unknown. Is it or isn't it a righteous wall pocket?
Without its metal frame, it's just a bottle but with the
frame it is made to hang on the wall and would make an
interesting addition to a collection of glass pockets. The
bottle was also made in clear and dark blue. The clear
and dark blue are being reproduced without the wire
frame. The old ones have a bar of music on the back
while the new ones seen by the author do not. This is
also sometimes seen with a metal frame holder that
includes a metal bow. These are sometimes found with
cold painted decoration that appears to be a factory finish. Estimated value: $25.00 to $35.00.*

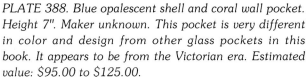

*PLATE 388. Blue opalescent shell and coral wall pocket.
Height 7". Maker unknown. This pocket is very different
in color and design from other glass pockets in this
book. It appears to be from the Victorian era. Estimated
value: $95.00 to $125.00.*

*PLATE 389. Aqua blue pocket with gold decoration.
Height approximately 7". Maker unknown. The decoration on this pocket is gold with tiny clear glass beads
over the gold. This gives the decoration a textured, three-
dimensional effect. This technique was used on Victorian
art glass and was known as coralene glass. This pocket
may be of later vintage. Estimated value: $40.00 to
$50.00.*

PLATE 390. Yellow glass pocket. Height 6",
mouth is 5" wide. U.S. Glass Company. The
background on this pocket is very much like
the crackle finish seen on PLATES 376 and
377. This pocket has the addition of curving
leaf shapes. It was pictured in a 1927 U.S.
Glass advertisement and was produced in
blue, green, and canary, the color shown. It
was also produced in satin finishes. Estimated
value: $35.00 to $45.00.

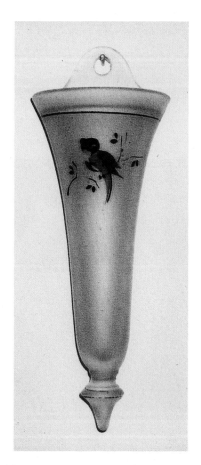

PLATE 391. Green pocket with parakeet. Height 9½".
Tiffin Glass Company. Tiffin referred to this as their
Jungle pattern. The glass has a satin finish. It was produced between 1922 and 1934. Estimated value:
unknown.

PLATE 392. Dark green with molded berries. Height
10¼". Maker unknown. The fluted edge on the top and
its round shape (it doesn't have a flat back), suggests that
this pocket may be of earlier vintage than many of the
other glass pockets pictured and could be from the Victorian era. Estimated value: $35.00 to $50.00.

*PLATE 393. Milk glass pocket. Height 7½", mouth 4½". Imperial Glass Company. This pocket is shaped somewhat like a whisk broom. In the 1950s, Imperial become a major producer of milk glass and this pocket is probably from that era. Estimated value: $25.00 to $35.00.*

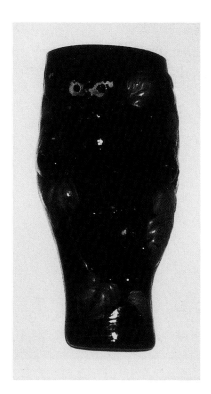

*PLATE 394. Owl pocket. Height 7½", mouth 3⅝". Maker unknown. This pocket is of black amethyst and the owl and leaves are molded in. The eyes and leaves appear to be cold painted. Estimated value: $60.00.*

*PLATE 395. Green glass pocket. Height 6", mouth 2". Maker unknown. This pocket has a fluted top and molded decoration that is very similar to PLATE 392. However, this is a much smaller pocket. Grape vines with leaves and grapes entwine this pocket. Like PLATE 392, it does not have a flat back. Estimated value: $35.00 to $45.00.*

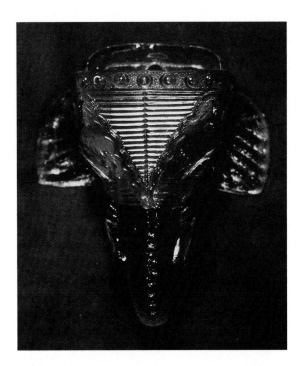

PLATE 396. Amber elephant. Height 5½". Made by the King Glass Company in amber, blue, and crystal. This was made before 1891, when King Glass Company and 17 other glass companies were absorbed by the U.S. Glass Company. Estimated value: $45.00 to $60.00.

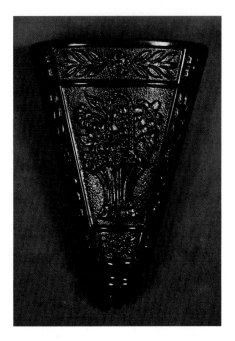

PLATE 397. Dark green pocket. Height 6". Maker unknown. Unlike many of the glass wall pockets from the Depression era, this pocket features considerable decorations. Its ornate decoration suggests that it may be from the Victorian era. Estimated value: $35.00 to $50.00.

PLATE 398. Green boot. Height 4¼". Maker unknown. This was a popular and fairly common holder for matches during the Victorian era. It was made in colors and clear. The ridges on the front were designed as a surface for striking matches. This particular pocket is a reproduction. Estimated value of reproduction: $10.00 to $12.00.

PLATES 399 & 400. *Glass silhouette pockets. Height 5¼". Maker unknown. These are similar to silhouette pictures that were popular in the 1940s. However, the glass has been bent to form a pocket. The back is made of cardboard so they were obviously not meant to hold water. Estimated value: $15.00 to $25.00 each.*

# Wall Pockets from Other Materials

Over the years, wall pockets have been produced in materials other than ceramics and glass. Wicker wall pockets were popular during the Victorian era. That was an era that valued crafts produced by the lady of the house. Wall pockets made from colorful postcards that were sewn or crocheted together with yarn were popular. Pockets with wood backs and needle-point fronts were produced by housewives and were used to hold a variety of items around the house.

More recently, wall pockets began to appear in metal. This was a popular material in the Arts and Crafts Movement from the early part of this century. Care should be taken in polishing old metal too zealously. The value of some metal pieces, especially bronze and metals from the Arts and Crafts period, is diminished by polishing away the original patina. Wall pockets made from brass and copper are still being produced and are readily available.

Plastic was invented in 1868, but it became a popular item for household products, most notably radios, between the world wars. After World War II, plastic items became very common in the home and in some cases began to replace ceramics and glass. Of course, plastic wall pockets were produced during that period. For many, they may be the height of kitsch. For others who find the 50s look charming and nostalgic, a grouping of plastic wall pockets may strike just the right decorating note. Older plastic pockets are not common but when found are generally inexpensive.

*PLATE 401. Wicker wall pocket. Height 18". The curls on this wicker piece suggest that it is from the turn of the century. As a rule, natural wicker is worth more than painted unless the paint is original to the piece. Estimated value: $75.00 to $95.00.*

PLATE 402. Wicker pocket with beads. Height 12". The beads incorporated into the design make this pocket with its ordinary shape much more interesting and desirable. Estimated value: $60.00 to $75.00.

PLATE 403. Bronze pocket (one of a pair). Height unknown. Unmarked. This is a beautiful old metal pocket that probably dates from the Arts and Crafts period. Unfortunately, much of the original patina has been polished away. The collector paid $42.50 for the pair but a similar pair was recently seen for $120.00.

141

PLATE 404. Metal flower pot with vines. Height 15". Unmarked. This looks like a flat wall plaque but it does have a narrow pocket. The pocket did not look like it would hold water, however. Estimated value: $15.00 to $20.00.

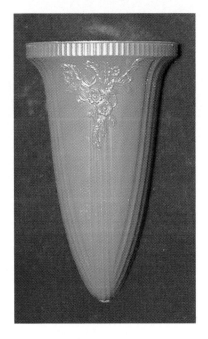 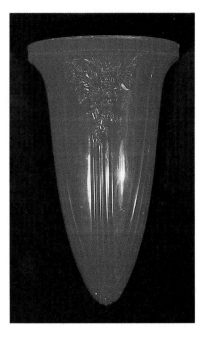

PLATES 405 & 406. Green and red plastic. Height 5¾". Mark: molded into the back, An Ardee Product, Made in the USA within a diamond shape. A 4 appears below the mark. I have also found this pocket in yellow. Estimated value: $5.00 to $7.50.

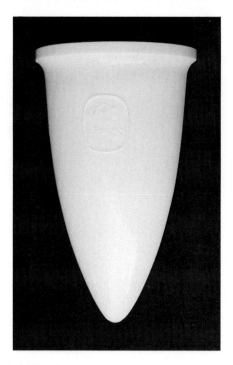

*PLATE 407. Cream plastic pocket. Height 6".
Unmarked. This pocket features a cameo of a profiled
woman in a bonnet with a parasol. Estimated value:
$5.00 to $7.50.*

*PLATE 408. Plastic silhouette teapot. Dimensions
unknown. Unmarked. Black and pink color were
popular color combinations during the 50s. This is
one of those decorative items that could be seriously
tasteless or quite delightful depending on the set-
ting. Estimated value: $5.00 to $7.50.*

*PLATE 409. Plastic silhouette coffeepot. Height 9¼".
Unmarked. This pocket appears to have been made by
the same company that made PLATE 408. The handles
on the pots and the finials on the lids are the same style.
A sugar bowl was also made in this series. Estimated
value: $5.00 to $10.00.*

*PLATE 410. Plastic silhouette of a man on a high
wheeler. Height 11" x 9" wide. This pocket was also
made with a white, rather than green, container. A
companion piece of a woman at a spinning wheel
was also produced. Silhouette pockets such as these
were produced during the 1950s. Estimated value:
$8.00 to $12.00.*

*PLATE 411. Plastic plate with roses. Height 7¾". Mark: paper label,* Hand Painted, Bernard Edward Co., Original, Chicago. *As the label states, the flowers on this copper colored pocket are hand painted. The pocket is behind the plate. Estimated value: $8.00 to $12.00.*

*PLATE 412. Blue plastic cup and saucer. Height 6". Mark:* Plas-Tex PT 883, Made in U.S.A. *The decoration on this pocket is an applied decal. Estimated value: $5.00 to $10.00.*

*PLATE 413. Green plastic cup and saucer. Height 4¼". Mark:* Made in U.S.A. *The decoration is hand painted. Estimated value: $5.00 to $7.50.*

*PLATE 414. Light green plastic cup and saucer. Height 5½". Mark:* A United Product, Made in U.S.A. *The decoration is an applied decal. Estimated value: $5.00 to $7.50.*

PLATE 415. *Green and red plastic cup and saucer. Height 7⅛". Mark: Maherware, 2, U.S.A. Estimated value: $5.00 to $7.50.*

PLATE 416. *Yellow plastic pitcher and saucer. Height 6". Mark: Worcester Ware, Made in U.S.A. The hand-painted decoration is flaking on this example. This is a little more unusual than the other cup and saucer pockets since it is a pitcher with a saucer. Estimated value: $10.00 to $12.00.*

PLATE 417. *Plastic cat. Height 5½". Unmarked. The cat has a little pocket in his head that may have been for kitchen matches. The hooks at the bottom were probably for potholders that came with it. It may have been sold as a kitchen gift set. Estimated value: $10.00 to $12.00.*

PLATE 418. *Plaster moon face. Height 5¼". Unmarked. This face looks like a cartoon of the moon popular in the 1920s. The small opening suggests that he may have been a match holder. He may have also been a room freshener with the perfume poured into the small pocket where it was absorbed into the plaster. It would then exude the fragrance back into the room. Estimated value: $15.00 to $25.00.*

# Unidentified Wall Pockets

I have tried to organize the wall pockets in this book by some sort of category — either by country or type. Of course, quite a large number of pockets defy such neat categorization. Many pockets are unmarked and it is not possible to identify them by other characteristics. What follows is a sampling of unidentified pockets, both cheap and expensive, that readers might find interesting.

PLATE 419. Pink and tan bird of paradise. Height 5½". Mark: impressed 8309. This pocket has a very nice art deco design. The clay body is white and it has two holes in the back. Some ceramics from Germany and Austria are marked with numbers. Estimated value: $15.00 to $20.00.

PLATE 420. Pink grapes. Height 6½". Unmarked. I have seen this pocket in other colors. The clay body is white. Estimated value: $10.00 to $15.00.

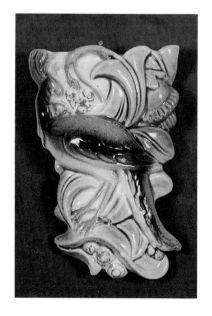

PLATE 421. Blue and tan bird of paradise (one of a pair). Height 5". Mark: impressed 8310. This pocket was obviously made by the same manufacturer as PLATE 419. Estimated value: $15.00 to $20.00 for one.

PLATE 422. Woman with roses. Height 7". Unmarked. This is a beautifully painted face with thin lashes and accented hair. I tend to think she was made in Germany but she could be Japanese. Estimated value: $20.00 to $30.00.

PLATE 423. White pocket. Height 6¾". Unmarked. This pocket has a rectangular molded ridge on the back that holds it slightly away from the wall. Estimated value: $10.00 to $15.00.

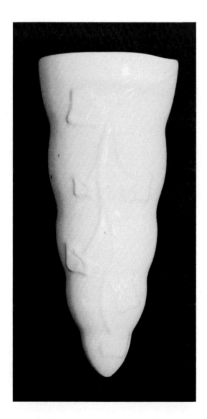

PLATE 424. White pocket with ivy. Height 7". Unmarked. This is probably an American-made pocket from the 40s or 50s. Estimated value: $10.00 to $15.00.

PLATE 425. Wagon wheel. Height 5¼". Unmarked. This has the look of the 1940s era American-made pottery. Estimated value: $20.00 to $30.00.

*PLATE 426. Blue pocket with roses. Height 7".
Unmarked. This pocket is probably American made. Estimated value: $15.00 to $20.00.*

*PLATE 427. Blue flower. Height approximately 5".
Unmarked. The glaze on this flower is reminiscent
of McCoy's "rustic" glazing used on their larger
flower wall pocket. Estimated value: $10.00 to
$15.00.*

*PLATE 428. Pink bow. Height 5½". Unmarked.
This pocket has a white clay body. There is a
large central hole and a smaller hole on either
side suggesting that it might have been used to
hold toothbrushes. Estimated value: $5.00 to
$10.00.*

*PLATE 429. Gold goblet. Height 7". Mark:
24K Gold, Made in USA. The glaze treatment is similar to a line produced by
McCoy. Estimated value: $20.00 to $30.00.*

PLATE 430. *Blue clock with gold trim. Height 7".* Mark: *24K Gold, Made in USA. This pocket was made by the same company that made PLATE 429. It was also produced with a black clock face and gold trim. Estimated value: $20.00 to $30.00.*

PLATE 431. *"Texas." Height approximately 5". Unmarked. Ordinarily I would consider this just a really tacky souvenir from Texas. However, given the interest in cowboy collectibles, I decided to include it. Estimated value: $5.00 to $10.00.*

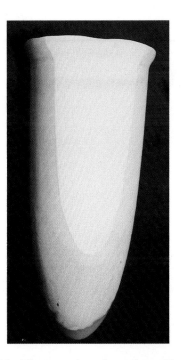

PLATE 432. *Green pocket. Height 5¾". Unmarked. This pocket is glazed front and back as well as on the inside. The upper rim is unglazed indicating that it was set in the kiln upside down on the rim to be fired. The glaze is reminiscent of green majolica glaze but rather thin. Estimated value: $10.00 to $15.00.*

PLATE 433. *Three colored pocket. Height 7½". Unmarked. This interesting three-color matte glaze treatment appears to be one-of-a-kind. This has the look of early art pottery. Estimated value: $25.00 to $35.00 (perhaps more if identified as the work of a major company).*

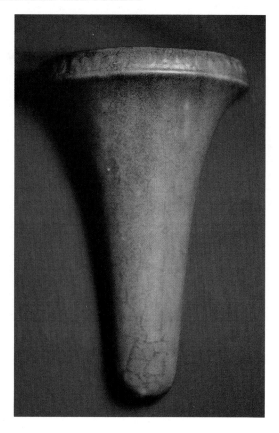

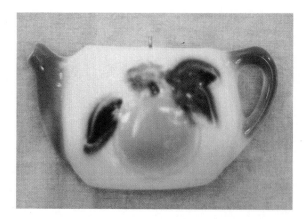

PLATE 435. Teapot with fruit. Height unknown (small). Unmarked. This little teapot was made in a variety of color combinations. The decoration was airbrushed. It is sometimes identified as a Shawnee product but I could not verify its maker after considerable research. Estimated value: $15.00 to $20.00.

PLATE 434. Green tapered pocket. Height 8". Unmarked. The dealer who had this pocket thought it might be early Roseville. The glaze looks like one of Weller's early glazes although several of the major art potteries produced a deep green matte glaze such as this. Dealer price: $198.00.

PLATE 436. White teapot. Height 6". Unmarked. This pocket was also produced with cold painted decoration over the white glaze. The painting is generally rather crude. Estimated value: $10.00 to $15.00.

PLATE 437. Teapot with clock face. Height approximately 4½". Unmarked. This little pocket was produced in several glaze colors and in white with gold decoration. Sometimes identified as a McCoy, its maker could not be verified. Estimated value: $10.00 to $15.00.

PLATE 438. Teapot with scene. Height unknown. Mark: 1201. This pocket is decorated with a decal depicting a couple in eighteenth century dress. It is trimmed in gold. Estimated value: $20.00 to $25.00.

PLATE 439. Teapot with strawberries. Height unknown. Unmarked. This has cold painted decoration and is part of a larger line of wall pockets with a kitchen theme featuring cold painted strawberries on a white background. This pocket has a mate that faces the opposite direction. Estimated value: $20.00 to $30.00.

PLATE 440. Teapot with blue flowers. Height unknown. Mark: Diamond Pottery. I could not find any information on the Diamond Pottery. Estimated value: $10.00 to $15.00.

PLATE 441. Hen. Height 5¼". Unmarked. This looks somewhat like the products of a number of American potteries that made wall pockets in the 1940s. Estimated value: $12.50 to $18.00.

PLATES 442 & 443. Ducks and cattails. Height 6½". Mark: Patented 149144. I found a similarly decorated ashtray marked Patent Pending, OPCO, Zanesville, O, USA. This was made by the Ohio Porcelain Company which made decorative wares from 1940 to 1956. The Ohio Porcelain Comapny may be the maker of these pockets. The facing pair on the right should be worth more as a pair than a pair facing the same way. These pockets were produced in a variety of glaze combinations. Estimated value: left, $10.00 to $15.00; right, $35.00 to $45.00 each.

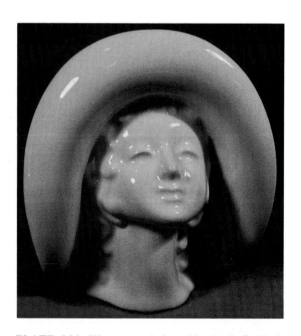

PLATE 444. Woman with hat. Height 5½". Mark: USA. Many companies marked their wares "USA," especially during World War II. It was patriotic then but confusing now. The popularity of head vases increases the value of this piece. Estimated value: $25.00 to $35.00.

PLATE 445. Light blue banded wall pocket. Height 6¼". Mark: Made in USA. This is another American-made pocket from the 1930s or 1940s. It has a nice art deco look to it. Estimated value: $15.00 to $25.00.

PLATE 447. Green arrowhead. Height 8". Mark: Creek with a stylized teepee. Estimated value: $20.00 to $30.00.

PLATE 446. Wishing well. Height 7½". Unmarked. This is a fairly common pocket that was also produced in green and rose. It was sometimes trimmed in gold. Estimated value: $10.00 to $15.00.

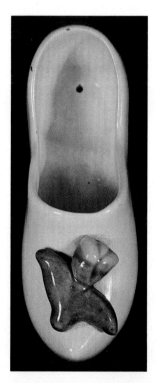

PLATE 448. White Dutch shoe. Height 8½". Unmarked. This is similar to a Dutch shoe produced by McCoy. The McCoy shoe is 7½" and the flowers are different. Estimated value: $10.00 to $15.00.

PLATE 449. Large clown. Height 10½". Unmarked. This looks like it was produced by a California pottery. Heidi Schoop, a California potter who worked in the 1940s, decorated her work in a similar manner. Estimated value: $35.00 to $45.00.

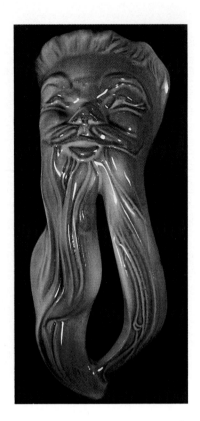

*PLATE 450. Cat. Height 13". Mark: Andrea, W-524. This cat is rather similar to cat wall pockets produced by Camark. The crackle glaze and surface decoration on this pocket has much more of an Oriental look to it, however. The pocket can be glimpsed under the cat's chin. Estimated value: $35.00 to $45.00.*

*PLATE 451. Man with beard. Height 10½". Unmarked. A light glaze was applied over a dark, terra cotta clay body to produce this glaze effect. Hull made a similar wall pocket but the beard was not as long on the Hull version. Estimated value: $20.00 to $30.00.*

*PLATE 452. Mosaic tile. Height 5". Unmarked. Broken tile and mirrors were combined to decorate this handmade wall pocket. The French call this type of decoration* picassiette *which literally means pickaxed plates. The pieces are held to the terra cotta body with an adhesive such as tile grout. Estimated value: $20.00 to $30.00.*

PLATE 453. Bananas and pear on leaves. Height 6¼". Unmarked. Wall pockets of fruit superimposed on leaves were very popular designs and were produced by several California potteries as well as McCoy. The stems on all of the unmarked fruit pockets shown in this section are different from the McCoy versions in the way the leaves and stems are modeled. Estimated value: $15.00 to $20.00 each.

PLATE 454. Pear and apple on leaves. Height 7". Unmarked. These appear to have been made by the same manufacturer who produced those in PLATE 453. The pears especially look the same but the leaves are a lighter green in this version and the pear has a bit more red on it. Note, however, that these pockets are ¾" larger than the previous pair. Estimated value: $15.00 to $20.00 each.

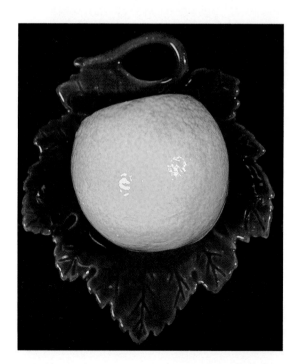

PLATE 455. Orange on a leaf. Height 7½". Unmarked. This pocket is even larger than the fruit in PLATE 454. The background leaves are also different. Estimated value: $15.00 to $20.00.

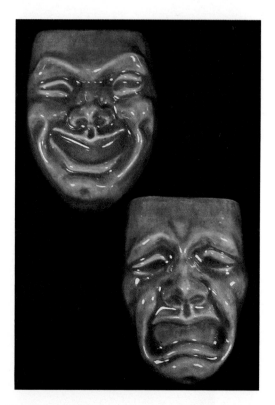

PLATE 456. Masks of comedy and tragedy. Height 6". Mark: Meyen Co. spelled backwards. Estimated value: $20.00 to $35.00 for the pair

PLATE 457. Red folk art vase. Height 5". Unmarked. This decoration is suggestive of that found in Mexican folk art. Estimated value: $15.00 to $20.00.

PLATES 458 & 459. Oriental man and woman. Height of man 11". Height of woman 9". These rather garishly decorated pockets look somewhat like chalkware. Cold paint decoration was airbrushed with the facial features hand painted. Estimated value: $15.00 each.

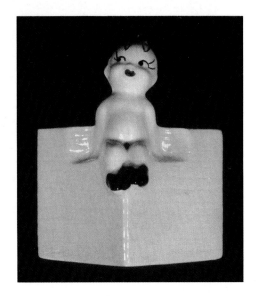

PLATE 460. Sitting elf. Height 4". Unmarked. Many California potteries produced wares decorated with elves and they may be the origin of this small pocket. Estimated value: $12.50 to $15.00.

*PLATE 461. Elf on a piano. Height 5". Unmarked. Given Californians' penchant for the mythical, I feel rather certain that this elf wall pocket was produced there. Estimated value: $20.00 to $30.00.*

*PLATE 462. Elf in cattails. Height 4". Unmarked. Estimated value: $15.00 to $20.00.*

*PLATE 463. Elephant in a hat. Height 7½". Mark: D inside larger D. This amusing pocket would be perfect for a child's room. Estimated value: $25.00 to $35.00.*

*PLATE 464. Calla lily. Height: 8". Unmarked. Estimated value: $15.00 to $25.00.*

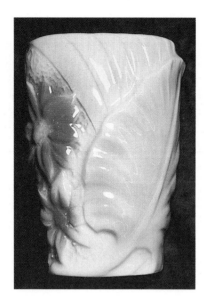

PLATE 465. *Flower and leaves. Height 5¾". Unmarked. This pocket was made in other color combinations. Estimated value: $15.00 to $25.00.*

PLATE 466. *Birdhouse. Height 7¼" x 4¾" wide. Unmarked. This is similar to the wares produced by a number of California potteries. Estimated value: $15.00 to $25.00.*

PLATE 467. *Kitten in a bucket. Height 6¾". Unmarked. The careful airbrushed decoration on this appealing pocket is reminiscent of the quality seen in Royal Copley wall pockets. Estimated value: $15.00 to $25.00.*

PLATE 468. *Renaissance man. Height 3¾". Unmarked. This small, undecorated pocket is made of porcelain. It has carefully modeled details. Estimated value: $15.00 to $25.00.*

# Bibliography

Bickenheuser, Gred. *Tiffin Glassmasters, Book II.*
    Grove City, Ohio: Glassmasters Publications, 1981.

Blayney, Molley. "Pick A Pocket!"
    *Country Victorian Accents*, April/May, Vol. 5, No. 1, 1993, pp. 28, 58, 60.

Chapman, Jack. *Encyclopedia of California Pottery.*
    Paducah, Kentucky: Collector Books, 1992.

Davis, Robert. Personal communication. April, 1994.

Gilson, Linda. "Wall pockets." *Our McCoy Matters*:
    *The McCoy Lovers Newsletter*, April/May, Vol. 5, No. 2, 1992, p. 9.

Hand, Sherman. *The Collectors Encyclopedia of Carnival Glass.*
    Paducah, Kentucky: Collector Books, 1978.

Hall, Doris and Burdell. *Morton's Potteries: 99 Years.*
    Morton, Illinois: Doris and Burdel Hall, 1982.

Huxford, Sharon and Bob. *The Collectors Encyclopedia of McCoy Pottery.*
    Paducah, Kentucky: Collector Books, 1982.

Huxford, Sharon and Bob. *The Collectors Encyclopedia of Roseville Pottery – Second Series.*
    Paducah, Kentucky: Collector Books, 1980.

Huxford, Sharon and Bob, eds. *Schroeder's Antiques Price Guide, 12th edition.*
    Paducah, Kentucky: Collector Books, 1994.

Karmason, Marilyn with Joan B. Stacke. *Majolica: A Complete History and Illustrated Survey.*
    New York: Harry N. Abrams, Inc. 1989.

Kovel, Ralph and Terry. *Kovel's Depression Glass and American Dinnerware Price List. 4th edition.*
    New York: Crown Publishers, Inc. 1991.

Lee, Ruth Webb. *Victorian Glass: Specialties of the Nineteenth Century. 1st edition.*
    Rutland, Vermont: Charles E. Tuttle Company, Inc. 1985. (originally published in 1944 by the author.)

London, Barbara and John Upton. *Photography. 5th edition.*
    New York: Harper Collins College Publishers, 1994.

London, Rena. "The Return of the Wall Pocket."
    *Antique Trader Weekly*, Feb. 18, 1979, pp. 54-55.

Mangus, Jim and Bev. *Shawnee Pottery: Identification and Price Guide.*
    Paducah, Kentucky: Collector Books, 1994.

McDonald, Ann G. *All About Weller.*
    Ohio: Antique Publications. 1989.

Musselman, Ellen. "The History of Art Pottery." Unpublished. Tyler, TX. 1993.

Roberts, Brenda. *The Collectors Encyclopedia of Hull Pottery.*
    Paducah, Kentucky: Collector Books, 1980.

Spillman, Jane Shadel. *The Knopf Collectors' Guides to American Antiques: Glass, Vol. 2,*
    *Bottles, Lamps and Other Objects.* New York: Borzoi Books, 1983.

Van Patten, Joan. *The Collectors Encyclopedia of Noritake – Second Series.*
    Paducah, Kentucky: Collector Books, 1994.

Weatherman, Hazel M. *Colored Glassware of the Depression Era.*
    Ozark, Missouri: Weatherman Glassbooks. 1982.

Weatherman, Hazel M. *Fostoria: Its First Fifty Years.*
    Springfield, Missouri: The Weathermans. 1982.

Weed, Clarance M. "The Useful Wall-Pockets."
    *House and Garden*, 39 (JAN. 1916), pp. xvi-xvii.

Wilson, Shea. "From Arkansas Clay: Carmark Pottery."
    *Antique Trader Weekly*, April 6, 1994.

Wolfe, Leslie C. and Marjorie A. *Royal Copley: Plus Royal Windsor and Spaulding.*
    Villa Grove, Illinois: Wolfe, 1983.

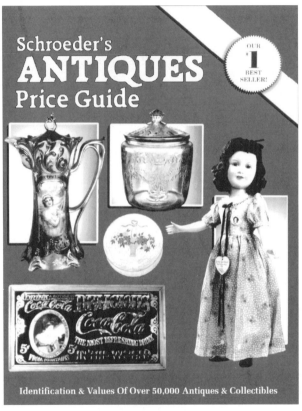